Menander: *Samia*

BLOOMSBURY ANCIENT COMEDY COMPANIONS

Series editors: C.W. Marshall & Niall W. Slater

The Bloomsbury Ancient Comedy Companions present accessible introductions to the surviving comedies from Greece and Rome. Each volume provides an overview of the play's themes and situates it in its historical and literary contexts, recognizing that each play was intended in the first instance for performance. Volumes will be helpful for students and scholars, providing an overview of previous scholarship and offering new interpretations of ancient comedy.

Aristophanes: Frogs, C.W. Marshall
Aristophanes: Peace, Ian C. Storey
Plautus: Casina, David Christenson
Terence: Andria, Sander M. Goldberg

Menander: *Samia*

Matthew Wright

BLOOMSBURY ACADEMIC
LONDON • NEW YORK • OXFORD • NEW DELHI • SYDNEY

BLOOMSBURY ACADEMIC
Bloomsbury Publishing Plc
50 Bedford Square, London, WC1B 3DP, UK
1385 Broadway, New York, NY 10018, USA

BLOOMSBURY, BLOOMSBURY ACADEMIC and the Diana logo are trademarks of Bloomsbury Publishing Plc

First published in Great Britain 2021

Cover image: Menander, Glykera, Spirit of Comedy (Komodia). *Ca.* 270 CE. Gift of the Committee for the Excavation of Antioch to Princeton University, y1940–435. © 2020. Princeton University Art Museum/Art Resource NY/Scala, Florence

A catalogue record for this book is available from the British Library.

Library of Congress Cataloging-in-Publication Data
Names: Wright, Matthew (Matthew Ephraim), author.
Title: Menander, Samia / Matthew Wright.
Other titles: Bloomsbury ancient comedy companions.
Description: New York : Bloomsbury Academic, 2020. | Series: Bloomsbury ancient comedy companions | Includes bibliographical references and index. | Summary: "This introductory companion offers a critical analysis of Menander's Samia for non-specialists. Matthew Wright brings the play to life by explaining how it achieves its comic effects and how it fits within the broader context of fourth-century Greek drama and society. He offers a scene-by-scene reading of the play, combining close attention to detail with broader consideration of major themes, in an approach designed to bring out the humour and nuance of each individual moment on stage, while also illuminating Menander's comic art. Menander's Samia is one of the best-preserved examples of fourth-century Greek comedy. Celebrated within antiquity but subsequently lost for many years, it miraculously came back to light, in almost complete form, as a result of Egyptian papyrus finds during the twentieth century. The play dramatizes a tangled story of mistakes, mishaps and misapprehensions leading up to the marriage of Moschion and Plangon. The young lovers' story is tied up with that of various other characters, including Moschion's father Demeas, Plangon's father Nikeratos, and above all Demeas' mistress Chrysis (the eponymous 'Woman from Samos'). For most of the play the characters are at odds with one another owing to accidental delusions or deliberate deceptions, and it seems as if the marriage will be cancelled or indefinitely postponed; but ultimately everyone's problems are solved and the play ends happily"– Provided by publisher.
Identifiers: LCCN 2020023397 (print) | LCCN 2020023398 (ebook) | ISBN 9781350124769 (paperback) | ISBN 9781350124776 (hardback) | ISBN 9781350124783 (epub) | ISBN 9781350124790 (ebook)
Subjects: LCSH: Menander, of Athens. Samia. | Greek drama–History and criticism.
Classification: LCC PA4247 .W75 2020 (print) | LCC PA4247 (ebook) | DDC 882/.01—dc23
LC record available at https://lccn.loc.gov/2020023397 LC ebook record available at https://lccn.loc.gov/2020023398

ISBN: HB: 978-1-3501-2477-6
PB: 978-1-3501-2476-9
ePDF: 978-1-3501-2479-0
eBook: 978-1-3501-2478-3

Series: Bloomsbury Ancient Comedy Companions

Typeset by RefineCatch Limited, Bungay, Suffolk
Printed and bound in Great Britain

Contents

Figures

Preface

Samia was the first Greek play I ever watched – in Evis Gavrielides' stunning production in the open-air theatre at Epidauros in July 1993 – and I have had a soft spot for it ever since. The play has a lot to offer. The plot construction, as in all Menander's comedies, is satisfyingly neat and tidy. The characters are subtle variations on familiar comic types. The presentation of ordinary domestic life in ancient Athens is full of interest. The situational humour is still easy to appreciate, even after nearly two and a half millennia. Menander's Greek is clear and straightforward. Unlike Aristophanes' comedies, this play can be read and enjoyed without an intimate knowledge of Greek history or a pile of commentaries at hand to explain all the obscure references. On top of all that, the fact that *Samia* was until recently a lost work makes it seem all the more enjoyable: we are amazingly lucky to have it at all. But it is still not among the better known or most popular ancient dramas.

This Companion sets out to bring this delightful play to a wider audience. All the material contained here is based directly on my experience of teaching Menander to undergraduates: it represents the distilled essence of countless lectures and seminars at Exeter and Vassar over the course of more than twenty years. Indeed, many of the ideas and interpretations outlined in the pages that follow are not purely my own, but have been developed through discussion and dialogue with students. Because this is so, it seems fitting to modify a standard cliché of academic prefaces. I wish to record my sincere gratitude to all my students, past and present, who have helped me to write this book. For any remaining errors that may be detected here, they can take the blame.

Note that all quotations from *Samia* are in English, using my own translations, but I have used the Greek text and line-numbering of Arnott's Loeb edition (except where otherwise stated).

M.E.W.
Topsham
Holy Week, 2020

Introduction

Menander's *Samia* ('The Woman from Samos') is one of a tiny handful of Greek comedies that survive from the fourth century BCE. For that reason alone it is enormously valuable to the cultural historian, as a rare example of a popular entertainment form and a glimpse into a fascinating but obscure period of ancient civilization. In addition, it happens to be a surprisingly fresh and enjoyable play which still has the power to make us laugh, in spite of its age and the considerable cultural gap that separates our world from that of Menander.

Samia is a funny, fast-moving comedy of mistakes, mishaps and misapprehensions, centring on the fraught events leading up to a wedding. The story of the two young lovers, Moschion and Plangon, is tied up with that of other central characters, including Moschion's adoptive father Demeas, Plangon's father Nikeratos, and above all Demeas' mistress Chrysis, the eponymous Woman from Samos. Everybody is eager that the wedding should take place. For most of the time, however, the characters are at odds with one another because of a series of accidental delusions or deliberate deceptions, and it seems as if the marriage will be cancelled or indefinitely postponed; but ultimately everybody's problems are solved, and the play ends on a celebratory note.

This Companion offers a critical introduction to the play and to Menander's comic art. It combines close attention to detail with broader consideration of important themes and modern scholarly approaches. More specifically, it aims to bring *Samia* to life by considering it primarily as a work in performance and showing how Menander makes this performance funny and engaging. The book will (I hope) be particularly suitable for students, teachers, actors, directors and anyone with an interest in the ancient theatre or the history of comedy.

How this book works

What follows is divided into five main chapters, one for each of the play's five acts. I move through the play sequentially, guiding the reader through the action in the order that it unfolds on stage. Throughout the discussion I try to evoke the sensation of watching a play in performance, and I write as if from the perspective of an audience member in the ancient Greek theatre. At every point I have kept two main questions in mind and tried to provide an answer (or to explain why a definitive answer is impossible). First: what can the spectators see on stage at this moment? And second: what do the spectators need to know in order to make sense of the play unfolding in front of them? A third, related question often has to be confronted: how does the experience of reading the play differ from that of watching it in performance?

For the purposes of the discussion I have broken each act down into 'scenes' (marked 'I.1', 'I.2', 'I.3' and so on). These are not formal act-divisions signalled in the script, but distinct units of action defined by the number and configuration of characters on stage at any given moment: each new 'scene' is marked by an actor's entrance or exit. Dividing the action up in this way helps us to concentrate our attention on the dynamics of the characters' interactions at each point. (Note that, owing to a theatrical convention current in Menander's time, there can never be more than three speaking actors on stage at once.[1] This odd restriction, which also applied to other forms of classical Greek drama, could be deliberately exploited for dramatic advantage in 'comedies of misunderstanding' such as *Samia*.)

Each chapter adopts the format of a scene-by-scene reading of the act in question. I begin by providing a brief description of what is said and done in each individual scene, before shifting the focus to carefully selected points of interest. As many others have observed, the dramatic effect of Menander's plays is hard to illustrate via plot summaries – it all depends on precise details and nuances. But at the same time, understanding the full significance of each detail usually requires us to consider broader issues of interpretation relating to the whole play and its genre. This is why I have structured the book in this way.[2] Essentially, it proceeds by 'zooming in' on specific small details and then 'zooming out' from these details to examine a related theme or more general question. I hope that the reader will thus be encouraged to understand what is happening on stage at any given moment as part of a bigger picture.

This is a short book, and it certainly doesn't claim to give exhaustive coverage of every conceivable aspect of *Samia* or its author. But it identifies and highlights the play's major themes, it offers a certain amount of critical discussion and interpretation (even venturing an original observation here and there), and it helps the reader to navigate the main currents in the scholarly literature. The notes in each section are primarily intended as signposts to further bibliography on all the topics mentioned, and an appendix contains a guide to further reading with a focus on general and introductory works.

The book is designed to make sense whether or not you have already read *Samia* itself. It is also designed to be read consecutively from beginning to end. Some of its arguments are cumulative, and some of its later sections refer back to points made earlier on. Nevertheless, it is not compulsory to read it in this way; I have also tried to provide basic assistance for readers who prefer to dip in selectively. Those in search of discussion of particular themes are directed to the Index (pp. 163–6), where principal topics are highlighted with an asterisk.

Ten things that you need to know

1. It is impossible to construct a reliable biography of Menander. How much do we need to know about an author's life in order to understand his work? The question is an open one (and the basic premises of traditional biographical criticism have been subjected to robust questioning by literary theorists), but it is still *de rigueur* for introductions and handbooks of this sort to begin with a brief biography. Unfortunately, almost nothing is known about Menander's life.[3] A few purportedly biographical details and anecdotes are preserved in a variety of ancient sources, but nearly all of them are demonstrably false or contradictory. (These sources are of interest to scholars for what they indirectly reveal to us about perceptions of Menander in antiquity, but they need not concern us here.[4]) All that can be said for certain is that Menander was an Athenian citizen; he was born *c.* 342–341 BCE; he started producing comedies at some point in the 320s; his first play was called *Orgē* ('Anger'); and he died *c.* 293–291. Some of the 'facts' reported in the anecdotal tradition are decidedly unconvincing – such as the detail that Menander at different times had mistresses called Thais and Glykera (who just happened to be the title characters of two of his comedies). Other details have been judged more plausible – such as the assertion that Menander's uncle was the comic poet Alexis, or that his friends included the philosophers Theophrastus (author of *The Characters*) and Demetrius of Phaleron (who was also the pro-Macedonian ruler of Athens from 317 to 307). But even these details may be fabrications. Mary Lefkowitz, in her *Lives of the Greek Poets*, shows that biographical 'facts' of this sort are usually extrapolated from the poets' works themselves: 'Like other poets, Menander was connected by his biographers with other famous literary figures, probably on the basis of perceived similarities in style and approach.'[5]

2. Menander was astonishingly prolific. We may not know much about his life, but we do know that Menander's literary output was enormous. The exact figure is subject to doubt, but he is credited with between 105 and 109 plays. In fact, Menander is far from being the most prolific Greek dramatist: he is easily surpassed by other fourth-century comedians such as Antiphanes (who is said to have written up to 365 comedies) and Alexis (who is credited with 245).[6] We cannot say whether the quality of these works matched their sheer quantity. Nevertheless, the fecundity of these writers has been attributed to the fact that they were writing within a genre that depended on the recycling of stock formulas and plot devices.[7] In this respect we could compare Menander to other 'genre writers' in more recent times, such as the thriller writers Georges Simenon and John Creasey or the romantic novelist Barbara Cartland (who wrote several hundred books apiece).

3. Menander is not Aristophanes. This may seem too obvious to be worth stating, but the fact is that most readers nowadays come to Menander after already having read some of Aristophanes' plays. It is easy to assume that both writers will be very similar. But Greek comedy was a diverse and flexible genre, and the two writers' comic styles are poles apart. Whereas Aristophanes' comedy is all about politics, current affairs and bizarre flights of fantasy, Menander's work is more realistic and centres narrowly on the everyday problems of domestic life. In contrast to Aristophanes' exuberant language, wit and verbal humour, Menander favours a more subtle form of situational humour based on character, misunderstanding and irony. The differences between the two playwrights are partly a matter of individual temperament: neither can be called a 'typical' Greek comedian. But another part of the explanation is that the comic genre kept evolving throughout the fifth and fourth centuries BCE. In between the death of Aristophanes and the beginning of Menander's career, a period of more than sixty years, the so-called 'Old Comedy' gradually transformed itself into 'New Comedy'. These terms, which seem to have been invented years later by Hellenistic scholars, are not entirely satisfactory, and modern critics still debate their exact meaning.[8] (In this book and elsewhere I prefer to use the label 'later Greek comedy'.) There are many continuities between fifth-century and fourth-century comedy, but it is undeniably true that the overall character of the genre had changed. Menander may not be entirely typical of his period, but he is not unique. The fragmentary remains of other fourth-century authors show that domestic comedy had overtaken political and fantastic comedy as the dominant form.[9]

4. Political circumstances shaped Menander's work. One of the causes commonly adduced to explain the transformation of the comic genre is that during the period of 'Old Comedy' Athens was a fully functioning democratic state, but throughout the fourth century the political situation was changeable and unstable. A major turning point was the defeat of Athens by Philip of Macedon in 338 BCE, followed by several decades of uncertainty. Throughout Menander's career, brief periods when democracy was restored alternated with longer periods of oligarchy under autocratic rulers installed by the Macedonians.[10] Some poets continued to write political comedy, but Menander seems to have deliberately avoided doing so – perhaps because he was a friend and associate of the pro-Macedonian Demetrius of Phaleron, perhaps because he favoured the Macedonian regime, or perhaps because he preferred to take refuge in escapism.[11]

5. *The performance venue and date of* Samia *are unknown.* As mentioned above, Menander's career stretched from the 320s to the 290s, so in theory *Samia* might have been produced at any time during that range. The fact that the play (unusually for Menander) contains a handful of topical references has sometimes been taken as evidence that it was a relatively early work, perhaps produced in the 310s, but this is uncertain.[12] Similarly, the festival at which *Samia* was performed is unknown. The closing lines of the play contain an appeal to the goddess Nike (Victory), who is described as sitting beside Dionysus at 'the finest of contests' (736). This description may perhaps be taken as a reference to the major dramatic festival in the Athenian calendar, the City Dionysia, but these lines constitute a standard formula, and their evidence is hardly compelling. Apart from the City Dionysia there were many other possible performance venues for a new comedy in Athens or Attica, including the Lenaea and the many smaller local Dionysia festivals (known as the 'deme' or 'rural' Dionysia) throughout the year; there were also many festivals further afield, across the whole Greek world.[13] It has been suggested that another reason for the disappearance of political content from Menander's plays in favour of 'universal' themes is that he envisaged his work as travelling far beyond Athens itself.

6. *Until very recently all Menander's plays were lost.* Ancient books were extremely fragile, and they could not survive long. In order for any ancient text to be preserved, it would have to be continually read and studied between antiquity and the modern period, and new copies would have to be made. This process of transmission often broke down

at some point over the centuries, even in the case of important authors. Even though Menander was one of the most widely admired poets throughout the classical period, his plays later disappeared without trace. Until the end of the nineteenth century, Menander's plays had the unenviable status of lost works, known only through fragments (i.e. quotations and references in other ancient authors whose works did survive). But then there followed a series of amazing archaeological discoveries in Egypt (where the warm, dry conditions underground enable the preservation of very old papyrus), as a result of which several of Menander's comedies were miraculously returned to the light of day. By the 1960s readers could once again enjoy a complete play (*Dyskolos*), two plays in a nearly-complete state (*Epitrepontes*, *Samia*), and substantial portions of a few others. The text of *Samia* was rediscovered in two stages.[14] Part of it (considerably less than half) was contained in a fifth-century CE book known as the 'Cairo Codex' (*P.Cairo* 43227), which was first published in 1907.[15] Subsequently the rest of the play (essentially complete, despite a few large gaps) turned up, along with *Dyskolos* and parts of *Aspis*, in a third- or fourth-century book known as 'Bodmer Papyrus XXV': the Bodmer text of *Samia* was first published in 1969, and is the main basis of all modern editions.[16]

7. Menander's plays are not 'classical literature'. These plays may be ancient, but they cannot strictly be called 'classics': the two terms are not actually synonymous, even though they are normally treated as such.[17] Even though Menander was rated very highly during the Hellenistic and Roman periods, his works later sank into total oblivion. Thus (in effect) these plays have only been around for a few decades; they have not had chance to exert a formative influence on later literature and culture (except indirectly, via Roman adaptations); they have never been part of the traditional Western canon; even now they seldom feature on educational syllabuses. In a sense, of course, the 'unclassic' status of Menander can be liberating for scholars and students. It means that we can approach his work unimpeded by the weight of accumulated opinion that attaches to other ancient authors, the product of long and complex processes of reception. In addition, it can make it easier for us to enjoy these comedies for what they are – well-made, mass-produced works of popular entertainment – rather than struggling to assimilate them to the intimidating category of Great Literature that the label 'classic' seems to imply.

8. *Menander's plays are very seldom performed.* In the years immediately after his rediscovery, when Menander was big news, there were several productions of *Samia* in Greece, Cyprus and elsewhere. Since then, there have been a few revivals, almost all of them small-scale and amateur productions in colleges and universities. As far as I can ascertain, *Samia* has never received a full-scale theatrical performance in Britain, though a version for BBC Radio Three (in a translation by Eric Turner) was heard in 1971, and a free adaptation by Chris Vervain (*Not The Same Old Samia*) was given a workshop performance in 2019. (Details of all known productions are preserved in the Oxford Archive of Performances of Greek and Roman Drama.[18]) The neglect of Menander by theatre producers is slightly mysterious, given that Greek drama remains generally popular with modern audiences. The most obvious reason for this neglect is that Menander's treatment of sexual relationships is undeniably offensive by today's standards, but this aspect of the plays could be glossed over in performance.[19] It is striking that Greek tragedies are nowadays staged far more often than comedies: perhaps this reflects a widespread perception that ancient humour is no longer very funny.

9. *Menander is funny.* (Oh yes, he is!) I have always found Menander hilarious, but, to my surprise, I have almost never encountered anyone else who thinks so. My students always complain that they don't 'get' him – at least, not at first. Now it may be that I am partly to blame for this, but every year the same students respond warmly to Aristophanes, Plautus and Terence; it is just Menander who leaves them cold. Epithets such as 'flat', 'dull', 'lame' or 'predictable' frequently make an appearance in essays and seminar discussions, along with descriptions such as 'Menander had no sense of humour' or 'all his plays are the same'. Even scholars who work on Menander often seem distinctly underwhelmed by his qualities as a comic writer. There is plenty of excellent literature

available on Menander's language and style, his dramaturgy, his characters, his social and intellectual themes, and so on, but most of it sidesteps the question of whether Menander's comedies are actually funny or enjoyable, as if such considerations were irrelevant or embarrassing. Similarly, whenever I tell my colleagues or other professional classicists that I am working on Menander, they often sigh or raise a satirical eyebrow, as if to say: 'Why?' Humour is, of course, a very personal and subjective phenomenon, and simply stating that something is funny doesn't make it so. But in this book I do my best to show why I think Menander is funny, despite the unenthusiastic responses of many readers.

10. Menander's comedy is based on formulas. The key to understanding Menander's humour is to recognize that all his plots and characters conform to a highly stylized set of generic rules. Those who complain that Menander's plays are 'all the same' are missing the point. The plays are *not exactly* the same, but they all resemble each other because they use the same basic ingredients time after time (young lovers who want to marry, old men at odds with their sons, troublesome servants, mistresses, money worries, family secrets, disputes over property and inheritance, illegitimate children, long-lost relatives reunited, predictable happy endings – and so on). The comic effect depends almost entirely on repetition and variation: the fun comes from seeing how a very limited fund of material is endlessly recycled, with inventive tweaks and modifications each time.[20] For this reason, formula-based comedy becomes funnier when you have seen or read a lot of it. If *Samia* is the first comedy of this sort that you have read, it will still make sense. But if you read a few other works of Menander, Plautus and Terence and then go back to *Samia*, it is more likely to 'click', because you will be able to recognize the formulas as such and appreciate how inventive Menander can be within the rules of the genre. The best way of illustrating this effect is to use analogies from other types of literature or drama where generic rules and formulas are equally important, such as the detective novel, the long-running television sitcom or the romantic comedy movie. When we open another Agatha Christie novel and see that someone has been murdered in mysterious circumstances, we do not tend to complain: 'Oh no, not *again*!' When we come out of the cinema, having seen a film such as *Muriel's Wedding, The Wedding Planner, The Wedding Date, My Best Friend's Wedding, Father of the Bride* or a hundred others along similar lines, we are unlikely to complain about the predictability of the ending. In all these cases, just as in Menander's comedy, familiarity with the conventions is crucial to the audience's enjoyment.

So much for introductory remarks. Now it is time to settle down and watch the show . . .

1

First Act

The comedy is about to begin! The spectators take their seats in the open-air theatre, talking among themselves while glancing down from time to time at the empty playing area (*orchēstra*) below.

We do not know where or when *Samia* was originally produced, but let us assume that the scenario under discussion takes place in the Theatre of Dionysus in Athens, at one of the Athenian dramatic festivals best known to us, the City Dionysia or the Lenaea. By the end of the fourth century BCE this theatre is a permanent, semi-circular stone structure, with more or less the same layout as can still be seen on the site today. The seating capacity of this theatre is well in excess of fourteen thousand.[1] Is it full, or nearly full, for the first performance of an exciting new work by Menander? It is hard to be certain. But we can be certain that the audience is making plenty of noise: these big Greek theatres are noted for their acoustic properties. It may well be that many of the spectators have already been sitting there for most of the day, watching other tragedies or comedies. If it is now evening, quite possibly some of them will have had too much to drink. In between the performances they may have taken the opportunity to stretch their legs, partake of refreshment or catch up on gossip with friends. We have to imagine a theatre bustling with noise, energy and movement.[2]

But now it is time to settle down quietly and pay attention to Menander's new play. How does the audience recognize the exact moment when the play has started? In a modern theatre there are usually clear signals to indicate that the world of the play has taken over from the real world – the dimming of the house lights, the raising of the curtain, the sound of the orchestra striking up an overture – but it seems that none of these conventions existed in the Greek theatre.

Probably the spectators gradually stop talking and start watching when they notice that an actor has entered the stage, either through one of the doors in the stage building (*skēnē*) or via one of the gangways (*eisodoi*) to the left and right of the *orchēstra*. They can see that this person is an actor, rather than an accidental intruder onto the stage, because he is wearing a theatrical costume and a mask. Nevertheless, the absence of a curtain or equivalent makes it seem likely that not everyone notices the actor's entrance immediately. Has the background noise entirely subsided by the time the actor starts speaking? Possibly not: in which case some of the spectators will inevitably fail to catch the play's opening lines.[3]

It is worth thinking carefully about these crucial moments at the beginning of the play – not just for the sake of making an imaginative effort to understand the experience of ancient theatregoers, or reminding ourselves of the importance of theatrical conventions, which differ widely between cultures and historical periods. These considerations are important whenever we contemplate ancient Greek drama, but they have a special significance in the case of *Samia* in particular. This is because Bodmer Papyrus XXV, the only surviving ancient copy of Act I, is missing several lines from the beginning. This is how it starts:[4]

...

] . . .ε. [.] υπερ[

]ονετι λυπῆσαί με δεῖ;

ὀδ]υνηρόν ἐστιν· ἡμάρτηκα γάρ.

. . . [*c. 7 missing lines; several unintelligible words or parts of words*] . . .do I have to cause distress [to myself *or* to someone else]? It's [pai]nful, for I have done wrong.

The fact that the papyrus is mutilated and lacunose at this point (as at many others) would normally be regarded as a serious misfortune. But, paradoxical though it may seem, one could argue that it actually brings us closer to the experience of Menander's original audience.

As modern readers we are accustomed to having neatly printed, complete playscripts to deal with: we experience them as texts, even if we attempt to approach them from a dramaturgical perspective, and we have access to contextual information to help us make sense of them. For instance, we see each character's name – in this case, MOSCHION – clearly printed in capital letters or italic script before the character himself has uttered a word. Theatre audiences, with only masks to guide them, have to wait for longer before the characters are fully identified (but see the next section for more on the signifying properties of masks). More importantly, readers of texts can pause and reread the first lines if they get confused. Theatre audiences have to work much harder to process the expository and scene-setting information provided at the beginning of a play. This is not true of ancient theatre audiences alone; it is an inherent part of the experience of any play in performance. The difficulty of 'the first five minutes' is a well-known phenomenon among contemporary audiences, especially when verse drama is being staged. As Nicholas Hytner writes (in *Balancing Acts: Behind the Scenes at the National Theatre*):

> 'Hang on in there,' I told the audience at a pre-show talk one evening. 'It gets easier.' Even with Shakespeare, the first five minutes are always a problem. I sit there thinking I have no idea what these people are talking about, and I'm supposed to be the director of the National Theatre.[5]

Considerations of this sort can give us a new perspective on the defective, fragmentary opening of *Samia*. If we miss a few words at the start of Moschion's prologue speech, or fail to grasp what he is talking about at first, could we not say that we readers are thus getting a more authentic 'theatrical' experience?

*

[I.1: *Moschion alone on stage*] *Moschion explains his background and his relationship with the other members of his household, namely Demeas, his adoptive father, and Demeas' Samian mistress Chrysis. Moschion reveals that he has fathered an illegitimate baby with Plangon, the girl next door, and announces that he wishes to marry her; but he can do so only with the approval of her father, Nikeratos, who is currently away on a business trip with Demeas (1–58).*

Mask and character

One of the most striking aspects of Menander's comedy, and one which distinguishes the plays from most other types of drama, is that all its characters wear masks. This fact can easily escape the notice of readers. Masks are never explicitly mentioned in the texts,[6] and even if we deliberately try to imagine the play in performance we are used to quite different conventions of acting on the stage or screen. The idea of masked performance probably strikes many of us as alien and distinctly odd. Ancient theatre audiences, by contrast, would have been long accustomed to watching masked actors. Masks invariably featured in all the Greek dramatic genres – tragedy, comedy and satyr-play – and their use seems to go back as far as the earliest origins of drama.[7] The symbolic significance of the mask may originally have had something to do with religious ritual, but the persistence of the convention probably owed more to practical considerations. Menander's comedies, like Greek tragedies, have a variable number of parts – *Samia*, with six speaking characters, has fewer than average – but the rules of the festival dictated that they had to be performed by a cast of only three main actors.[8]

Nevertheless, the precise function of masks changed and developed during the classical period. By the late fourth century, it appears that comedians were using a system of standardized masks, each of which denoted a particular type of character. This meant that the spectators, if they were familiar with the different mask types, would have been able to tell at a glance whether the actor standing in front of them was playing the part of an old man, a boastful soldier, a cook, a prostitute, a slave, or whoever it might be. Thus when the actor playing Moschion enters the stage at the start of *Samia*, it is immediately apparent because of his mask that he represents not just any character but a young man.

But how do we know all this? There are two main sources of evidence for these comic mask types. The first is the *Onomasticon*, a lexical work compiled by the Roman scholar Julius Pollux in the second century CE. This is sometimes dismissed as a late and not entirely trustworthy source, but it is generally accepted that Pollux drew on earlier scholarship, including the treatise *On Masks* by Aristophanes of Byzantium.[9] The *Onomasticon* (4.143–54) contains a detailed list and discussion of forty-four comic masks, which I summarize here:

Old men

1. *the first grandpa* (cropped hair, placid features, beard, lean cheeks, white face)
2. *the second grandpa* (leaner, more serious and troubled-looking, sallow face, beard, red hair, cauliflower ears)
3. *the leading old man* (head crowned with hair, hook-nosed, full in the face, one eyebrow raised)
4. *the long-bearded, wavy-haired old man* (like 3, but with a longer beard and no raised eyebrow; sluggish appearance)
5. *the Hermonios* (receding hairline, full beard, raised eyebrows, fierce expression)
6. *the pointy-bearded old man* (like 6, with a different beard; difficult-looking expression)
7. *the Lycomedeian* (curly hair, long beard, one eyebrow raised, interfering expression)
8. *the pimp* (like 7, but smiling; brows contracted, bald or receding)
9. *the second Hermonios* (clean-shaven, pointed beard)

Young men

10. *the thoroughly admirable youth* (ruddy, athletic, tanned; full head of hair; raised brow)

11. *the dark youth* (younger than 10, no raised brow, studious-looking)
12. *the curly-haired youth* (younger than 11, ruddy, curly-haired, brow wrinkled)
13. *the delicate youth* (younger than 12, hair like 10, white face, delicate-looking)
14. *the rustic* (dark features, thick lips, snubbed nose, head crowned with hair)
15. *the first wavy-haired youth* (boastful soldier type; dark skin and hair)
16. *the second wavy-haired youth* (like 15, but more delicate and fair-haired)
17. *the flatterer* (dark skin, hooked nose, easy-going, raised eyebrows)
18. *the parasite* (like 17, with battered ears and a more cheerful look)
19. *the portrait-like* (grey hair, clean-shaven, well-dressed, foreign)
20. *the Sicilian* ('a third parasite', presumably like 17; description is missing)

Servants

21. *the grandpa* (white hair; denotes freedman status)
22. *the leading slave* (red hair, raised eyebrows, screwed-up forehead)
23. *the low-haired* (like 22, with a receding hairline)
24. *the curly-haired* (red hair and skin, balding, cross-eyed)
25. *the slave Maison* (bald and red-haired)
26. *the 'cicada'* (black skin, a few tufts of black hair, black beard, cross-eyed)
27. *the wavy-haired* (like 22, with different hair)

Old women

28. *the wrinkly old woman or 'little she-wolf'* (long, wrinkly face, white hair, sallow, squinting)

29. *the fat old woman* (wrinkly, fat; hair tied up with ribbon)
30. *the little housekeeper or 'sharp old woman'* (snub-nosed, lacking teeth)

Young women

31. *the chatterbox* (hair round the face, brow unwrinkled, white skin)
32. *the curly-haired* (like 31, with different hair)
33. *the maiden* (hair parted, straight black eyebrows, white face)
34. *the first false maiden* (paler than 33, hair tied up at the front; resembles a bride)
35. *the second false maiden* (like 33/34, but with hair unparted)
36. *the greying chatterbox* (grey hair; signifies a retired prostitute)
37. *the concubine* (like 36, but with hair flowing round the face)
38. *the mature prostitute* (like 34, with redder complexion and curly tresses)
39. *the little prostitute* (unadorned; hair bound with ribbon)
40. *the golden prostitute* (hair adorned with much gold)
41. *the prostitute with a scarf* (colourful scarf around head)
42. *the 'little torch'* (hair plaited at the top so as to resemble a torch)
43. *the favourite handmaid with cropped hair* (cropped hair, white girdled robe)
44. *the smooth-haired slave girl* (hair parted, snub-nosed, scarlet girdled robe)

There is some doubt about exactly how this list should be interpreted. Do these forty-four mask types represent the entire range of possibilities available to a comedian in Menander's time (or later)? Do they reflect a completely standardized, universal system, or did every theatrical company have its own unique collection of masks, corresponding broadly to the categories above but differing from one another in precise details? Can every character in Menander be matched up to one of the forty-four types? Scholars have disagreed considerably about how to answer these questions.[10]

They have also disagreed about how to reconcile the evidence of Pollux with our second major source, consisting of assorted archaeological remains. The perishable materials from which they were made ensure that not a single original mask survives from a comic production, but it happens that theatregoers throughout the Hellenistic and Roman worlds were fond of collecting theatrical memorabilia and souvenirs, which tend to be more durable. We are lucky enough to possess many ancient replicas and depictions of masks, in stone, pottery, mosaics, paintings and other media. (Nearly all such artefacts have now been catalogued and discussed by T.B.L. Webster, J.R. Green and A. Seeberg in their essential reference work *Monuments Illustrating New Comedy*.) The most valuable by far, because they are exactly contemporary with Menander, are a large collection of miniature models of comic masks excavated from a cemetery on the island of Lipari in 1879. More than four hundred of these painted terracotta masks are known, and various attempts have been made to match them up with the forty-four mask types in the *Onomasticon*. Luigi Bernabò Brea, for instance, writes of 'the perfect correspondence between the catalogue's descriptions and the masks found in Lipari', and sees this correspondence as evidence for the existence of a fully fixed typology in Menander's time.[11] By contrast, Joe Park Poe judges that the Lipari masks and other monuments do not fit Pollux's scheme closely, and that the *Onomasticon* reflects not a standardized system but just a broadly representative selection, or maybe the inventory of the properties of one particular theatrical troupe.[12] The most balanced general account can be found in *Monuments Illustrating New Comedy*, where Pollux and the Lipari masks are discussed side by side with other relevant artefacts, but more evidence is needed before the question can ever be resolved conclusively.

Even if we assume that Pollux's forty-four mask types are more or less identical to the masks available for use in the production of *Samia*, we still do not know precisely which mask was worn in the case of each character. For instance, any of the types 10 to 13 might in theory seem suitable for Moschion, though type 10 in particular (the *panchrēstos* or

Figure 1 Terracotta mask probably representing Pollux's character type 34 (the *pseudokorē*), *c.* 325–300 BCE. From the Lipari collection (Lipari, Museo Eoliano). AKG Images.

'thoroughly admirable young man') has frequently been identified as the most likely choice. The two older men, Demeas and Nikeratos, might have been represented by a pair of contrasting masks from types 3 to 7. The name Chrysis, which means something like 'Goldie', might seem to suggest mask type 40 (the *diachrysos hetaira* or 'golden courtesan'), but Chrysis' status as the live-in mistress of Demeas probably means that type 37 (the *pallakē* or 'concubine') is more suitable. Any of types 22–4 or 27 might do for the slave Parmenon, and types 25 or 26 for the cook.[13] One could while away a pleasant few minutes going through the cast list of every comedy in this way and trying to match all the characters to mask types, but this would be no more than an exercise in guesswork. Unless one believes that the mask was a signifier of essential character traits (rather than a basic indicator of identity and type), it probably doesn't matter exactly which mask was used in each case.[14]

It has sometimes been suggested that each specific mask type may have been associated with a specific named character, just as in the *commedia dell'arte* tradition, where the same stock characters (Arlecchino, Il Dottore, Pantalone and so on) recur time after time in different performances.[15] Was the character Moschion a recurrent character of this sort, immediately recognizable by means of a special 'Moschion mask' each time? Certainly there are other young men called Moschion in Greek comedy (for example, in Menander's *Sikyonios* and *Perikeiromene*), and we know that at least some other character names (including Demeas, Parmenon, Chaireas, Chairestratos and Smikrines) were reused by Menander in more than one play. But if there really had been a standard 'Moschion mask' and a 'Demeas mask' (and so on) in regular use, it is suspicious that neither Pollux nor anyone else in antiquity ever mentions the fact. Furthermore, a careful look at the plays one by one shows that, although they may share names, these characters differ distinctly from one another in their traits, and the way in which they come across through their words and actions turns out to be subtly variable.[16] Even if some names or masks might initially suggest certain stereotypical attributes, the plays are interesting – and funny –

precisely because of the discrepancy between predictable stereotypes and the more complex, rounded characters that we actually encounter. Menander likes to play around with our expectations; he also likes to depict real people, not two-dimensional stock characters.[17] On the whole, then, comparisons with *commedia dell'arte* do not really illuminate Menander's characterization.

Masks are undoubtedly an important part of comic stagecraft. They may not be the key that unlocks the entire meaning of a character, but they contribute to a distinctive aesthetic, they are associated with highly stylized performance techniques, and they make it possible for the audience to recognize at a glance the general type of person that the actor is playing. In the case of Moschion, the mask tells us his age and gender. But not all young men in comedy are exactly the same. If we want to find out more about this one we have to listen to what he says next.

Moschion's prologue (or speech for the defence)

On the basis of the title we might be expecting that Chrysis, the 'Woman from Samos', is going to be the principal character, but that would be a mistake (and in fact the titles of Greek comedies don't work like that).[18] It is Moschion who is the main focus of attention from the start. I hesitate to use the word *hero*, partly because the idea that a play has to have a 'hero' would have been unfamiliar to Menander, but mainly because Moschion cuts such an unheroic figure.

As we listen to his opening speech, what strikes us immediately is its downbeat tone. Greek and Roman comedies often use the opening monologue not just as a convenient way of explaining the story so far (a technique that owes a great deal to Euripidean tragedy) but also as a sort of 'warm-up act', a means of generating humour and getting the audience in the right mood before the main action starts.[19] However, Menander seems to favour a relatively austere narrative format for his prologues, and there is certainly a shortage of laughs in this one. The mood is subdued. Moschion is not just supplying background information for the spectators' benefit; he is making a confession.

This young man is palpably shifty, hesitant, ill at ease. His first intelligible words are 'distress' and 'painful' (2–3). He openly admits 'I have done wrong' (3), though a little later he is too embarrassed to tell us in so many words what he has done ('I shrink from saying what happened next', 47). He delivers his account in a syntactically jerky style, stopping and starting mid-flow, asking questions to himself or to the audience, and repeating himself. He keeps saying 'perhaps' (26, 47), suggesting doubt or indecision in his mind. He uses the verb 'to be ashamed' four times (*aischunomai*, 23, 27, 47, 48). This is a man preoccupied by guilt.

The monologue or soliloquy delivered to an empty stage is a familiar dramatic convention, commonly seen throughout tragedy and comedy. The technique flouts strict realism, of course, but it is a convenient way of enabling a character to communicate their inner thoughts to the audience. Nevertheless, characters in comedy – in marked contrast to tragedy – sometimes deliberately draw attention to the artificiality of the convention by openly acknowledging the presence of an audience. By doing this the actor self-consciously reminds us that he is an actor and that the world he inhabits is a make-believe one.[20] This can have a strangely disorientating effect whenever it occurs in a prologue, because it acknowledges the presence of the audience before any consistent dramatic world has been established. Throughout his speech here Moschion keeps directly addressing us (5–6, 19–20, 49), and he even tries to create a sense of intimate confidentiality between himself and us ('I can say this because we are all by ourselves', 13).[21] No doubt the actor uses gestures, body language and the appearance of eye contact as well as his words to draw us in. This is just the sort of communicative technique that many other comic prologue speakers use, but in this case the style and content of Moschion's speech make it seem more than just a standard attention-grabbing device.

The fact that the main character is telling the story himself (rather than an omniscient divine narrator or a character less directly involved) makes a big difference. In effect, we are listening to a speech for the defence. Moschion is not just narrating the backstory; he is pleading for our sympathy and understanding, and he seems to be treating us as if we were jurors trying his case.[22] When Moschion turns to us and calls us 'Gentlemen' (*andres*), he is using a mode of address familiar from the law court. Exactly as a defendant might do, Moschion carefully establishes his previous good character (13–16), drawing attention to his exemplary public service as a theatrical producer (*chorēgos*) and cavalry commander (*phylarchos*) and his generosity to the poor and needy. He subsequently supplies a narrative of the facts in the case as he sees them (20–57), and admits his own culpability ('The guilt is mine, I did not deny it', 50–1). Thus in both its structure and its style this speech clearly echoes forensic oratory of the period.

The effect is striking but far from unique: in fact Menander and other Greek dramatists quite often exploit the similarities between the act of watching a play and the act of sitting in a court or assembly.[23] Nor is this the only scene in *Samia* where the characters address the audience using legal language: Demeas' monologue at the start of Act III employs precisely the same sort of tactics (207–79) when he invites the audience/jury to consider a case of alleged adultery with himself as the victim. All these echoes of the law court are worth noting because they represent just one way in which Menander's comedies, though often described as apolitical, are embedded within an identifiable historical and civic context.

Kosmios and other evaluative terms

What sort of person is Moschion? We will keep learning more about him as the rest of the play unfolds, but by the end of his opening speech we have discovered several important facts about his character and status. He is young; he is rich; he is a prominent Athenian citizen. He is the adopted son of Demeas, with whom – on the surface, at least – he enjoys a good and affectionate relationship. But what about his inner personality or ethical disposition? Since Menander is often associated with a special (or indeed seriously philosophical) interest in characterization and ethics,[24] it is important to pay attention to any explicitly evaluative words and phrases that his characters use to describe themselves and one another. At the same time, we cannot assume that these evaluations are altogether accurate, bearing in mind not only the pervasive presence of human error and misunderstanding in these comedies but also, in many cases, the inherent ambiguities of language.

On line 18 Moschion describes himself as *kosmios.* This is an interestingly vague word, which is variously translated in English as 'well-behaved', 'good', 'proper', 'decent', 'respectable' or 'seemly'. It may refer to either outward behaviour or inner character; it may suggest piety, self-restraint and conformity to societal norms, but it could also suggest an excessive concern for outward appearances or the good opinion of other people; it could even hint at a troubling propensity for dissimulation or dishonesty. Note also that Demeas later on uses exactly the same word (twice – at 273 and 344) to describe Moschion. Do both characters mean exactly the same thing when they use the word? Is it meant to seem arrogant or egotistical for Moschion to use the word when describing himself? Is it supposed to have positive or negative connotations? What does it imply about Moschion's true nature, or his relationship with Demeas? The answers to these questions are debatable, and different scholars have interpreted the word, and the character himself, in a variety of contrasting ways.[25] But perhaps it is unnecessary to look for a single definitive explanation. We may well conclude that Menander has deliberately made it difficult for us to evaluate Moschion. As I have already said, characters who are entirely black and white are few and far between in this type of drama; it seems that Menander would rather give us interestingly variegated shades of grey.

Sex and the R word

'I have done wrong', confesses Moschion (*hēmartēka,* 3); but what exactly has he done? It is a little while before he elaborates on this statement, and even then, in his great embarrassment, he falls back on another ambiguous form of words. Moschion explains (38–49) how he encountered the girl next door, Plangon, when she and her mother came to his own house to celebrate the nocturnal Adonia festival. This was a private ritual for women only, which meant that Moschion should not have been present at all.[26] Nevertheless . . .

> as you might imagine, there was plenty of fun going on at the festival. The women's noise made it rather difficult for me to sleep, so I managed to infiltrate the party and – oh dear! – I sat watching them. There were women here, there and everywhere, bringing Adonis-gardens up to the roof, and dancing, and celebrating their all-night revels. I shrink from saying what happened next – maybe I'm unduly ashamed, but I am ashamed none the less. The girl became pregnant.

So this is what it's all about: a sexual liaison outside marriage, with unplanned consequences. Or was it rape?

This poses an enormous problem for a modern reader or theatre producer. Sex is inevitably a sensitive and emotive subject, but attitudes to sex and gender are so culture-specific that almost any language that we use is likely to be problematic. Even if Moschion had been more explicit about what happened up on the roof, his way of describing it would not have corresponded to modern discourses of sexual morality. Trying to decide, on the basis of his evasive language, whether we should refer to this particular sex act as 'rape', 'seduction' or something else is not actually a very helpful activity.[27] No matter what our personal attitude or our own cultural background may be, we have to be hyper-alert to the fact that Menander and his contemporaries constructed sex and sexual relationships very differently from us.

The most important factor to bear in mind, which highlights an astonishing difference between ancient Greece and modern Western societies, is that female consent to sex was not usually regarded as the central issue at stake. If someone like Moschion had sex with a woman outside marriage, whether or not she was a willing partner, what counted above all was whether she was a citizen capable of producing legitimate children; and if anyone's rights were seen as being violated, it was the woman's family or, more specifically, her male protector (*kurios*).[28] In Athenian legal discourse 'rape' would fall under the general heading of crimes of *hubris*, but there is no ancient Greek word corresponding to 'rape' in English. Even if Moschion is what we would call a 'rapist', he would not have described himself as one. He certainly acknowledges that he has behaved badly, but he does not seem to regard Plangon as his 'victim'; what troubles him is the thought of his own father's reaction rather than the feelings of the girl and her family (61–9). It is also assumed that he can put things right by marrying the girl, just as soon as he obtains her father's consent (which, as we shall see, is freely given). The emphasis is on respectability and the production of citizen offspring, rather than the wishes, desires or emotions of Plangon herself. But there is no doubt that we are meant to see this outcome as a happy ending.

Could it be, then, that it is too distracting or anachronistic to use the R word in connection with Menander? To do so can make it seem as if Menander shared our own vocabulary and values. Perhaps we need some other word less heavily burdened with associations: a neutral-sounding phrase such as 'problematic extramarital sex' might be more appropriate. But RAPE? The word shouts out, drawing attention to itself. It is an ugly, shocking word, denoting an act that we have come to see as one of the most appalling of crimes. Even using the word itself can feel almost like committing a violation or uttering an obscenity.[29] The idea that anyone could write a *comedy* about rape, or that anyone could find such a comedy funny or relatable, is a very difficult one to entertain. But much of the sex in Menander, Plautus and Terence falls into this category,[30] which shows that these comedians and their audiences saw it, time after time, as a perfectly acceptable topic for humorous treatment. Even scenarios involving violent sexual assault (as in *Epitrepontes*) were deemed acceptable. At the risk of introducing another anachronism, we could say that the rapes in comedy function in a way roughly analogous to the murders in detective novels. They are treated as a crime serious enough to be worth all the fuss, they tell us a lot about the values of the society that produced them, they are a necessary device to set the plot in motion, and they represent a problem that is always resolved in the end. But they are evidently not designed to make us feel outrage or disgust.[31]

No wonder, perhaps, that these plays are seldom performed nowadays. Any director who does attempt to stage *Samia* for a modern audience will have to find a way of confronting – or skating over? – the central problem of sex and the R word. But more than any other feature of Menander this problem reminds us that when we adapt ancient comedies for the modern stage we are translating cultures, not just words.[32]

*

[I.2: *Chrysis, Moschion, Parmenon*] *After a lacuna in the text, we see Chrysis on stage: she welcomes Moschion and his servant Parmenon, who bring news that Demeas and Nikeratos have returned home. Parmenon urges Moschion to tell Demeas immediately that he wishes to marry Plangon. Meanwhile Plangon has given birth to a baby, but a plan has been made to deceive Demeas into thinking that Chrysis is the baby's mother (58–86).*

How will it all end?

This is where the fun starts. The opening scene – together with what we know of the rules of the comic genre – sets up certain expectations and makes us speculate what is going to happen next. We know that some things are definitely not going to happen, because they would break the rules. Some scenarios can be discounted at once: Moschion is not going to end up in prison; Demeas is not going to find himself a boyfriend; Chrysis is not going to marry the cook; no one is going to die. Things like that never happen in Menander's comedy. Other things sometimes do: for example, perhaps Moschion and Plangon will turn out to be long-lost siblings, just like the sweethearts in *Perikeiromene* . . . but no, that will not work here, because we already know that Moschion and Plangon have had sex, and incest (as opposed to narrowly averted incest) is the stuff of tragedy, not comedy. But (as Sherlock Holmes almost said) when you have eliminated the impossible, what remains is the truth – or, at least, what remains is a finite but expansive range of amusing possibilities.[33] The enjoyment for the audience lies in seeing exactly which of the possible outcomes will happen, and in savouring the way in which it all comes about.

We can be pretty certain that Moschion and Plangon will eventually get married, because the fate of a citizen child is at stake and because that is how these marriage plots always end. Even though most of Menander's plays, or their endings, are lost, it is inconceivable that any of them featured a marriage that was anticipated but infinitely deferred: it would be like a detective novel where the identity of the murderer was never revealed. The situation is funny precisely because the outcome is never in doubt. Indeed, one of the main sources of humour throughout *Samia* arises from seeing how the marriage keeps being postponed, even though we know that every single person in the play wants it to happen. Unlike certain other comedies where people deliberately put obstacles in the way of the young couple, in *Samia* all the delays and difficulties arise because of human error and bad luck. In each successive scene Menander carefully arranges things so that the characters are at cross purposes. At any given point in the plot, right up to the last moment, at least one character is always at odds with the others because of a misunderstanding. The comic effect lies in the timing and the precise ordering of these crucial moments of misapprehension or recognition. We enjoy the eventual happy ending not just because of our emotional investment in the characters' situation but also because of the satisfying neatness with which Menander has put it all together.

One way of thinking about audience expectations and possible plot outcomes involves the concept of 'Chekhov's Gun', often invoked by directors or critics in connection with modern stage productions. The concept derives from Anton Chekhov, who famously stated: 'One must never put a loaded gun on the stage if it isn't going to go off.'[34] This principle is conspicuously not observed by Menander. In fact, what he does often represents the exact opposite. Early on in the plot he will introduce a 'loaded gun', in the form of a familiar formulaic motif with a predictable outcome, and then deliberately not make anything of it. Act I of *Samia* features several 'loaded guns' which never go off. The fact that two of the leading characters (Demeas and Nikeratos) are on a business trip overseas suggests various plot possibilities, all of which are paralleled in other Greek or Roman comedies. Will they make a significant discovery while in Pontus? Will they encounter a new character there? Will they make or lose a fortune, or suffer a shipwreck on the way home? In fact, as we shall see, none of these eventualities arises, and the two old men simply return to Athens without further ado. Still more tantalizing is the fact that the natural parentage of both Moschion and Chrysis is unknown. This sets us up to expect astonishing revelations about their identity and origins, as in many another comic scenario. Is Chrysis really a Samian by birth? Might she turn out to be the daughter of an Athenian citizen, lost or abandoned at birth? Is she actually related to one of the other characters? Why is so much emphasis placed on the fact that Moschion is an adopted son? Why is nothing said about the circumstances of his birth or adoption? Why (unless it was mentioned in one of the lost sections) are we never told whether Demeas ever married or had any children of his own? Anyone who understands how formula-based comedy works is bound to run through a list of possible outcomes in their mind. Menander is perfectly well aware of all this, but, having teased us by raising our expectations, he leaves all these plot strands dangling and never develops them at all. This is what Stanley Ireland calls 'the comedy of disappointment', and it is central to Menander's comic technique, not just in *Samia* but elsewhere.[35]

Of course it is impossible to be certain that the cognitive processes experienced by Menander's spectators were exactly as I have imagined here. But we can usefully compare the experiences of a group of readers somewhat closer in time – those scholars who attempted conjectural reconstructions of *Samia*'s plot in the years before 1969. For both types of audience, ancient and modern, educated guesswork was called for, even if it usually turned out to be wrong. For instance, Edward Capps, writing in 1910, based his reconstruction on the hypothesis that the play featured two babies: not only the child of Plangon but also the child of Chrysis, disguised as a foundling.[36] Francis Allinson, the editor of the 1921 Loeb edition of Menander, suggested that 'the story of the Samian girl, who gives the title to the play, may have been made very prominent in the missing acts'.[37] Körte and others favoured a scenario in which Chrysis would turn out to be an Athenian citizen, possibly the natural-born sister of either Moschion or Plangon, and would subsequently form a legitimate marriage with Demeas at the end of the play.[38] A.W. Gomme, whose 1936 article discusses and rejects most of these other proposals, imagined a plot in which Plangon herself played a part in delaying the wedding by refusing to marry Moschion.[39] All of these reconstructions were falsified by the rediscovery of the papyrus text; but all of them were entirely plausible.

Parmenon and the master–servant relationship

Up to this point the play has not exactly been a barrel of laughs, but the first entry of the slave Parmenon lightens the mood. Slaves in comedy are often the funniest characters, and Parmenon is no exception. He is less cunning and crafty than many of his counterparts in other plays (even though Demeas describes him as 'more meddlesome than anyone else' 300), and he does not play a decisive part in determining the course of events (unlike, say, the slaves in *Perikeiromene* and *Aspis*, both named Daos). Nevertheless, he is a recurrent source of humour as well as an effective foil figure to his hapless young master Moschion. In general, comic slaves (rather like P.G. Wodehouse's Jeeves) are presented as being cleverer and more authoritative than their hapless masters. This is a very obvious inversion of social norms, though it would be hard to read it as a serious critique of existing power structures or the institution of slavery; it is simply funny because it is part of the incongruous, topsy-turvy world of comedy.[40]

Our first encounter with Parmenon reveals that, whatever his other qualities may be, he is an extremely *bad* servant – insolent, belligerent and bossy. Even as he enters the stage, he is in the middle of an argument. When Moschion asks, 'Did you see my father?' he replies: 'What? Are you deaf? Yes, I did!' (61–2). It is clear that Parmenon is the one giving the orders here: he tells his master that he has to 'act like a man' (63–4) and inform Demeas that he wants to get married, and he goes on to issue specific instructions for the wedding preparations (70–6). When Moschion admits that he is nervous, Parmenon not only raises his voice at him but insults him, using the abusive term *androgynē* ('hermaphrodite' or 'pansy', 69), a word which combines sexual mockery with an accusation of cowardice.[41] He is shouting so loudly at this point that he is reprimanded by Chrysis ('Why are you yelling, you wretch?'). Even by the standards of comic servants, this is remarkably unservile behaviour.[42] It provides a bit of light relief after the sombre prologue-cum-confession speech, but it also serves to emphasize what a weak, dismal figure Moschion is. He may give the impression of being a successful, upper-class Athenian gentleman, and it may flatter his ego to think of himself as *kosmios* (see above), but he needs this rude slave to put him in his place and tell him how to behave.

Chrysis, mistress and mother

During the same scene Demeas' mistress Chrysis, the eponymous Woman from Samos, has also made her first appearance. Unfortunately, the state of the text is so poor that we are missing not only Chrysis' own opening speech but also Moschion's description of her part of the backstory. Between lines 56–7 (where Moschion is just about to describe what happened to Chrysis 'a little while ago') and lines 58–9 (where Chrysis catches sight of Moschion and Parmenon returning from the harbour) there is a large lacuna in the papyrus. Thus we are deprived of certain vital pieces of information, as well as the chance to hear Chrysis' own perspective on events and relationships within the household.

What we know from the earlier part of the prologue (21–9) is that 'Demeas fell in love with a courtesan [*hetaira*] from Samos', that this love affair made Demeas feel so embarrassed that he kept it secret, and that Moschion found out and urged Demeas to make the arrangement more permanent because younger rivals were vying for Chrysis' attentions. All of that information, together with the play's title, may initially lead us to expect that Chrysis is going to be a stereotypical courtesan, wrapping Demeas round her little finger, and that the plot is going to centre on the sexual rivalry between Demeas and her other clients. After all, there were already dozens of earlier '*hetaira* comedies' along similar lines and with nearly identical titles, including *The Woman from Boeotia* (by Antiphanes, Diphilus and Theophilus), *The Woman from Ephesus* (by Antiphanes), *The Woman from Leukas* (by Amphis, Alexis, Diphilus and Menander), *The Woman from Achaea* (by Alexis), *The Woman from Cnidus* (by Alexis and Menander) and many others; there was even an earlier comedy called *The Woman from Samos*, by Anaxandrides.[43] As in many other ways, familiarity with comic tropes and formulas shapes the audience's expectations of what is to come. But quite apart from all these comic precedents, the very mention of 'a woman from Samos' would have made many of Menander's spectators call to mind the sex trade, for the island of Samos was famous in classical times for its prostitutes, one of whom, Philainis, was credited with the authorship of the world's first manual of sexual techniques.[44] Is Chrysis going to conform to the stereotype?

As we shall see from her later appearances, the answer is no – or not entirely. But for the moment let us concentrate on first impressions. It would be useful to know exactly which mask the actor playing Chrysis is wearing (see above, pp. 17–20), because it would make a big difference to our initial perception of her character whether one of the 'prostitute' masks (types 38–42 in Pollux) or the *pallakē* mask (type 37) is being used.[45] Alas, we can only guess. But what we do know for certain is that when Chrysis appears she is nursing a baby. In fact, *every* time we see Chrysis she has the baby in her arms. This baby is both a significant 'prop' throughout the play and a crucial feature of Chrysis' characterization.[46] (It is likely that a doll was used on stage rather than a real baby, which could not be relied upon to keep silent when required.) Like the mask, this prop functions semiotically to identify and define Chrysis' role, but it means that the main visual signal she gives off is maternal rather than sexy: this makes a big difference to how we respond to the character.

In order to persuade Demeas and Nikeratos to let Moschion marry Plangon, it is thought best to conceal the fact that Plangon has given birth; thus it comes about that Chrysis pretends to be the mother of Plangon's baby. This is a silly, impractical plan, doomed to failure. Perhaps we are just supposed to go along with it, rather than stopping to think about it too much. Because of the lacuna, it is impossible to be certain whose plan it was. However, it has normally been assumed that Chrysis herself hatched the plan, and that she did so partly out of the kindness of her heart but partly because she had recently lost (or had been compelled to give up) a baby of her own.[47] Some or all of this must have been made explicit in the lost lines. Even if Chrysis' motivation was not spelt out in full, it must have been made clear that she had given birth to a baby. But was Demeas the father? Was it exposed at birth, did it die, or was it given away? The answers to these questions remain mysterious to us.

Even if Demeas was the baby's father, and even if the baby had survived, its presence in the household would have been severely problematic. Not only would it have made ambiguous the status and rights of Demeas' adopted son Moschion,[48] but it would have been illegitimate and, as the child of a foreign woman, it could never have been recognized as a citizen. Considerations of this sort are crucial in Menander's world, where all newborn children, even if their status is initially in doubt, are eventually confirmed as *bona fide* Athenian citizens. This outcome is apparently non-negotiable within the rules of the genre: like the marriage of young virgins to their rapists, it is a necessary precondition of comedy's happy endings. Indeed, Menander's recurrent preoccupation with legitimacy, marriage, inheritance and related matters has been interpreted as a powerful expression of

Athenian civic ideology, in response to those who have seen his plays as inhabiting a depoliticized world of pure escapism.[49]

The inconvenient offspring of Chrysis is out of the picture, then, and its bereft mother is left not only holding but suckling Plangon's baby (78–9). Are we supposed to treat Chrysis' loss lightly? Surely her predicament should evoke sympathy rather than indifference; it also makes it easy to understand why she agrees so readily to the suggestion that she should pretend that she is the other baby's mother. She evidently wants a baby very badly. Chrysis confesses that she can't bear the thought of giving this baby up, and she claims, too confidently, that she will easily be able to persuade Demeas to accept the situation (80–6):

> He will soon stop being cross, because he's in love, dear boy – he's caught the bug just as badly as you've caught it yourself – and love very quickly makes even the most irascible man come to terms! For my part, I think I would endure anything at all before handing over this baby to a wet-nurse in some housing block . . .

Alas, Demeas does not love her as much as she imagines, so she is proved wrong; but that makes her situation seem all the more poignant. As so often in Menander's comedies, the humorous and absurd aspects are accompanied, or undercut, by more sombre elements. Chrysis is getting herself tangled up in a farcical plot, but we also get a glimpse of real pathos and human feeling not very far beneath the surface.

*

[I.3: *Moschion alone*] *After another lacuna, we find Moschion delivering another monologue: he expresses despair and decides to go away somewhere in search of solitude (87–95).*

Moschion's suicide threat

In between the holes in the papyrus we observe Moschion describing himself as wretched. By this time we will have been struck by his relentless self-absorption: he is concerned exclusively with his own feelings. When he cries out, 'Shall I not hang myself right away?' (91), it is tempting to imagine one or two of the rowdier audience members shouting back at him: 'Yes! Go on, then!'

His threat of suicide, even though it could be seen as a sincere *cri de coeur*, is actually much less affecting than the previous scene involving Chrysis, because we know that it will never be translated into action. Moschion now seems to think that he is a character in a tragedy, where hanging is a fairly frequent method of suicide – albeit one that was seen as dishonourable and associated exclusively with women.[50] But men don't hang themselves, and men in comedy don't ever die. So by uttering this empty threat Moschion just shows himself up as silly and self-dramatizing.

It's worth observing that suicide is a topic that is treated very lightly by comedians. Other references to suicide in comedy are all exploited for broad humour – as in the case of the soldier in *Perikeiromene* who vows to throttle himself after a tiff with his lover, or the man in one of Philemon's plays who breezily announces his wish to hang himself in order to be able to meet the long-dead Euripides.[51] Are jokes about suicide inherently funnier, or less shocking, or less offensive, than jokes about rape? It's hard to give a straightforward answer to that question, but it is none the less important to keep taking note of the variety of types of humour, and the range of different tones, that Menander uses in a single short scene.

Now Moschion exits the scene in search of 'some lonely spot' (94), and until the entrance of the next characters we are left to contemplate the empty stage again for a few moments.

*

[I.4: *Demeas, Nikeratos and mute servants*] *The two old men return from abroad. In the course of desultory conversation it emerges that they have already agreed to the marriage of Moschion and Plangon (96–119).*

Demeas and Nikeratos as a comic double act

The entry of the two new characters marks yet another shift in tone. Nikeratos and Demeas are simultaneously long-standing friends, next-door neighbours and business associates, and very soon (if all goes to plan) they are to become relations by marriage as well. The two old men come on stage mid-conversation, and immediately we notice several things about them. First of all, their dialogue is trivial and apparently irrelevant to the plot. A pair of grumpy old men, complaining about the horrors of travel and the beastliness of being abroad: this is the type of inconsequential banter that we often find at the beginning of Aristophanic comedies, but it comes as more of a surprise here, especially after the prevailing gloom and anxiety of Act I.

The second thing we notice is that Demeas and Nikeratos make a distinctive comic double act. This term, though its meaning will probably be clear enough, needs a bit of preliminary definition. Many scenes in *Samia* and elsewhere involve two characters engaged in some sort of confrontation or conflict, and such contrasts function as an important method of characterization in a general sense.[52] But not every binary contrast or combination is a 'double act' as such. There are just a few character pairings that seem to stand out as unusual: Demeas and Nikeratos are such a duo. They always appear either together or in parallel scenes.[53] In their appearance, temperament and mode of speech, and in the way they interact with one another, the friends form a complementary and contrasting pair. The fact that they both represent the same basic character type (old man) is important, because it makes the differences all the more pronounced. Demeas is rich; Nikeratos is comparatively poor. Demeas is the more articulate speaker, whereas Nikeratos prefers short, sharp outbursts.[54] Demeas is cleverer and more even-tempered, while Nikeratos is simpler and more irascible.[55] (These differences in speech and behaviour are not all equally apparent from their first appearance on stage, but they will become increasingly obvious in the successive scenes that follow.) Differentiated mask types will have been used, probably a contrasting pair from Pollux's 'old man' group (types 3–7: see pp. 14–21 above). Presumably the costumes also differed, but it has additionally been suggested that Demeas is fat and Nikeratos is thin.[56] This is impossible to prove, but the physical contrast would work well on stage. It would give a nicely ironical edge to the criticism of the 'fat old men' (98) who populate the Black Sea region, and it would underline the similarity of this double act to Stan Laurel and Oliver Hardy.

The old men's scenes together contain more jokes per line than the other bits in between. That is not to say that their dialogue is altogether side-splitting – this is still a play by Menander, after all, not Aristophanes or Plautus. But it is striking that their exchanges feature irrelevant, light-hearted material that seems to be there simply for its own sake, to make us laugh, rather than for the sake of the plot. This particular scene starts off with a tirade against the Black Sea region and its inhabitants (96–100):

> So now you're really aware of the change of scene – how different this place is from the horrors there! Pontus – fat old men! Tons of fish! Awful business! Byzantium – wormwood! Everything bitter! Oh God!

It is not certain who is speaking which lines here. Most editors assign the whole lot to Demeas, but the asyndeton of lines 98–101 (from 'Pontus . . .') looks very like the 'staccato' style used by Nikeratos elsewhere.[57] In a sense, it hardly makes any difference, since the two men share the same sort of outlook on the world. Now these lines are funny partly because they have nothing to do with the tangled affairs of the miserable Moschion (which means that they come as a refreshing change), and partly because they play on conventional xenophobic prejudices (which means that everyone can find the joke amusing whether or not they share those prejudices: they either laugh *with* the speaker or *at* him). But rather more simply, many people just enjoy watching cantankerous elderly gentlemen moaning about something. It's hard to explain exactly why this should be so – deep psychological and sociological causes could be adduced, no doubt – but it is a seemingly universal source of humour. Menander understood this well

– which is why his character Knemon in *Dyskolos* ('The Cantankerous Man') is so memorable – but the basic situation is familiar from many other types of comedy across different cultures.

When the slaves have been sent inside with the luggage, we might well be expecting the plot to get moving again, but Nikeratos is unwilling to drop the subject of foreign travel. He continues in a similar vein (106–9), expressing his amazement that the fog in Pontus was so thick. Demeas comes back with a punchline (110–11): 'No indeed – there was nothing there worth seeing! That's why the sun shone on the people there as little as it could get away with!' As Alan Sommerstein points out, this gag is as old as Homer (a version of it appears in the *Odyssey*),[58] but Demeas and Nikeratos are not people for whom a joke easily loses its first freshness. In fact Nikeratos even repeats the same witticism later on, at the end of Act III ('Demeas must be mad! The Black Sea isn't a healthy place', 416–17). This is a rare example of what comedians nowadays refer to as the 'callback' technique, whereby a detail that might seem insignificant gains in meaning and becomes increasingly funny through repetition; it is a way of creating links and associations between different parts of a performance, increasing overall coherence, or exploiting audience goodwill from the memory of jokes that got a laugh the first time round.[59] The technique is particularly associated with stand-up comedy and improvisation, which is why it is surprising to see it at work in Menander.

The wider world outside

It can sometimes seem as if Menander's fictional world is completely self-contained, with no topical references or explicitly political content. By and large this is true, and it is one of the main ways in which Menander contrasts with Aristophanes and fifth-century comedy. The explanation may have something to do with changing tastes, or a feeling that Athens under oligarchic or Macedonian rule was no longer a favourable environment for political drama, or the fact that comedies were increasingly designed to be 'exportable' for performance all over the Greek world.[60] Certainly *Samia* has no political message for its audience, it is devoid of any content that could be seen as controversial or offensive, and it requires no special knowledge of the historical context to understand and enjoy it (in contrast with Aristophanic comedy, which calls for at least one footnote per line).[61] That is why, in the absence of any external evidence, it is impossible to attach a definite date to the play. Nevertheless, *Samia* does occasionally make us aware of a wider world beyond its imaginary Athenian street scene, and a wider set of concerns beyond private domestic problems. Throughout this chapter I have drawn attention to several ways in which this is done, such as the emphasis on Moschion's record of public service, the highly artificial use of law-court rhetoric, and the play's underlying ideological focus on Athenian citizenship and identity politics. Elsewhere in the play we see other little glimpses of the contemporary world – most notably in Act IV, where three real-life Athenians are mentioned by name.[62] All of this is done with the very lightest of touches; it is easy to miss it.

At the end of Act I there is another brief acknowledgement that there is a real world outside. In the middle of his rant against overseas travel and foreigners, Demeas breaks off and exclaims: 'Dearest Athens! If only things could turn out for you as you deserve! That way we who love the city could live a completely blessed existence' (101–4). This passage is particularly interesting because it may be the closest that Menander ever comes to protesting about his political circumstances. Here he is not just acknowledging an external reality but even going so far as to admit that Athens has problems. All the same, this vague comment seems half-hearted, to say the least. What are these problems? Are they political, social or economic in nature? How can they be solved? Demeas does not tell us, nor does he even hint at a more specific meaning or target for criticism. This shows just how far we have come from the world of Aristophanes, in which someone like Dicaeopolis or Trygaeus would tell us exactly who was responsible for these problems and offer a brainy idea for solving them. Certain scholars have suggested that Demeas' words contain a cryptic allusion to a specific political crisis (such as the aftermath of the Lamian War of 322 BCE and the subsequent impoverishment of Athens), but there is no way of knowing whether this is true.[63] In any case, as the play's most recent commentator points out, 'at virtually *any* time in Menander's career it would be true that Athens did not have the power or prosperity that most Athenians would consider she deserved'.[64] Even if there is a specific reference underlying Demeas' words, it is important not to overemphasize the level of political engagement here. This perfunctory, wishy-washy utterance does not really qualify as an expression of protest, and I think it would be misguided to present Menander as having a definite political point to make (as if that could make him seem a more interesting or edgy writer). All that needs to be stressed is that Menander is not writing completely in a vacuum. His plays are products of a specific time and place, and if we look carefully we can see signs of this.

2

Second Act

Act II is the most badly damaged portion of the play, with many lacunae and incomplete or unintelligible lines. It is not always possible to tell exactly what is going on, but it is obvious that three important plot developments take place. First, Demeas reacts to the revelation that Chrysis is (as she claims) the mother of the baby. Second, Demeas tells Moschion that he has already arranged for him to marry Nikeratos' daughter, thus saving Moschion from having to make any embarrassing confessions or pleas. Third, Demeas for some reason persuades Nikeratos that the wedding should take place immediately.

Between the acts

In between the end of each act and the start of the next there is a break, during which we are treated to a display of singing and dancing. Manuscripts tend to denote the presence of a choral interlude with the stage direction *CHOROU*, an abbreviation for '[performance] of the chorus'. The stage direction is sometimes missing because of a lacuna, as here, but it is present after *Samia* lines 420 and 615 and in several other Menandrean papyri.

This stage direction has almost always been interpreted as meaning one of two things: either that the chorus performed a song-and-dance routine without any lyrics, or that the lyrics were not thought to be an integral part of the play.[1] In either case, it is presumed that the music and/or words must have been composed by someone other than Menander, and that such interludes must have been considered inessential to the play's meaning or impact. Scholars who have interpreted the stage direction in this way have linked it to Aristotle's discussion, in the *Poetics,* of what he calls *embolima* ('inserted songs'), defined as 'sung parts that have no connection with the plot'.[2] In numerous textbooks and commentaries one reads about the 'reduced importance' of the chorus in the fourth century, and it is common to encounter the view that all song-and-dance routines in comedy of this period were entirely perfunctory, functioning merely as a formal device to break up the conventional five-act structure.[3]

In fact, as Lucy Jackson has recently shown in a major reassessment of the evidence, this traditional view of the fourth-century dramatic chorus is highly questionable. In the first place, not only is Aristotle's discussion of *embolima* unclear but also its application to Menander is problematic (Aristotle is talking about particular examples of tragedy, not comedy or all of drama).[4] Even more importantly, fragments from Menander's contemporaries and rivals suggest that the chorus did not dwindle at this time, but continued to flourish. Comic titles such as *The Chorus* (by Epicrates), *Builders* and *Female Choreuts* (by Posidippus) and *Scythians* (by Antiphanes) indicate that the identity and function of the chorus was at least sometimes important, while several comedians evidently gave the chorus an active participatory role in the plot and dialogue.[5] Menander himself took some care to distinguish the specific identity of his choruses from play to play: they might be drunken young revellers (as in *Samia*), or hunters (in *Hero*), or Pan-worshippers (in *Dyskolos*).

Even if it could be shown that Menander did not exploit the chorus to maximum effect, there is no reason to treat him as typical or representative of the entire comic genre in this period. But why should we assume that Menander did not make substantial use of the chorus? Obviously he preferred not to give the chorus members any speaking parts in the scenes of dialogue, or any interaction with the main characters; but this does not mean that he gave them nothing else to do. As Jackson demonstrates, that crucial stage direction *CHOROU* is ambiguous. It does not necessarily have anything to do with so-called *embolima* (whatever Aristotle may actually have meant by that term).

Nor does it imply that the choral odes were unimportant, or that specially composed songs did not exist, or that they lacked words, or that they were irrelevant to the plot or themes of the play, or that someone other than Menander wrote them, or that they were 'merely' act-dividing interludes. All *CHOROU* indicates is that whoever copied out the text excluded the choral portions. One can imagine a variety of possible reasons why this might have occurred, arising from the habits of ancient scribes, readers or actors. Our manuscripts of Greek drama almost always omit the musical notation, even when they do include the song lyrics: this seems to have been a normal convention of the transition from performance script into book form. Among our surviving fragments of ancient books we possess several examples where choral odes alone have been excerpted and transmitted independently of the dialogue portions, or rehearsal texts containing only selected parts, or manuscripts that use the direction *CHOROU* where original choral odes definitely did exist (such as in Aristophanes' later plays).[6] In other words, it is perfectly possible that, despite the gap in our text, Menander did write original lyrics and music for the chorus to perform between the acts.

None of this, admittedly, helps us very much in the absence of any further evidence. All we can do is try to imagine what the choral interludes *might* have sounded like. Our general knowledge of ancient Greek music allows us to be fairly confident about the instrumentation that would have been used – including the double *aulos* (a reeded woodwind instrument, similar to the modern bassoon or oboe), pan-pipes, drums, castanets, tambourines and other percussion – as well as the aesthetic style of choral lyrics in this period. If words accompanied the music they would be sung in unison, their metrical pattern corresponding to the musical rhythm, and the tune would be composed in one of a limited range of modes (corresponding roughly to keys in modern Western notation), such as the Aeolian, the Dorian, the Phrygian or similar.[7] It is impossible to know exactly how this sort of music sounded, but we do possess a few valuable scraps of ancient musical notation as well as other literary and archaeological evidence, and on this basis modern scholars have made limited attempts at reconstruction. Readers wishing to investigate the subject further will find plenty of information and entertainment in Ernst Pohlmann and Martin West's collection *Documents of Ancient Greek Music* (which facilitates performance by presenting ancient musical scores and modern transcriptions side by side) as well as Armand D'Angour's website and documentary 'Rediscovering Ancient Greek Music' (which includes recordings of 'authentic' performances).[8]

If the chorus did sing specially composed lyrics, it is easy to imagine ways in which their content may have been linked to the preceding scene. Perhaps they explicitly commented on the characters or their situation, or perhaps they took the form of general reflections on themes such as the power of love. (For an example of how this type of free-standing but thematically relevant ode might work, we could compare the choruses in any of Seneca's tragedies.) Even if we prefer to stick with the traditional view that the choral sections were wordless *entr'actes*, we should not downplay the importance of 'irrelevant' interludes of this sort from the theatre audience's perspective. It is easy for readers and scholars to overemphasize the verbal and textual aspects of a play, partly because the text is all that we have left. But the power of drama does not depend entirely on words, literal meanings and 'relevance'. The non-verbal, aesthetic and emotional aspects are just as important – and the fact that such aspects are much harder to identify or reconstruct does not mean that they can be ignored.

Even if the choral interlude contained no words, and thus no explicit connection to the plot, it is certain that it would have affected the audience's reaction to the preceding act. The interlude gives us time to process what we have just seen on stage, now that all the main characters have been introduced. It allows us time to speculate what will happen next and to form our own (potentially mistaken) assumptions – which, as I explained in the last chapter, is a big part of the pleasure afforded by Menander's comedies. It creates a pause in the structure and rhythm of the plot: audiences cannot be expected to concentrate intensely for ninety minutes at a stretch, so they need a carefully maintained balance between tension and relaxation. It significantly manipulates our emotional and cognitive response to a scene, since music has a huge influence on mood. Perhaps we could think of Menander's music as functioning in much the same way as incidental music in modern cinema: whether this is specially composed or a carefully curated soundtrack of pre-recorded music, it is 'irrelevant' in an interpretative sense, but it can significantly change our experience of a scene or a key moment; it can even establish the entire character of a film. So it may be in this case too. Is the music slow or fast, loud or quiet? Does it evoke particular memories or associations? Which instruments and musical modes are used? Is the overall effect sad, reflective, exuberant? Is there a lively pulse or beat? How much percussion is there? What style of choreography is used? All these factors are bound to make a difference to how we view the characters and their situation.

But most importantly of all, the music and dancing are designed to be entertaining and enjoyable in their own right. My own abiding memory of Evis Gavrielides' production of *Samia* at Epidauros in 1993 is of the extraordinary music and choreography. The style of the whole production, including the scenes of dialogue, was designed to bring out the play's farcical side, and the music was composed to reflect this light-hearted mood: it sounded noisy, jaunty and jolly, with an 'oompah'-type accompaniment. The chorus, kitted out incongruously in black pinstriped suits and bowler hats, like butlers in an English stately home, entered the stage on bicycles; but in their later appearances they swapped bicycles for prams and wheeled the prams about the *orchēstra* in interweaving figures of eight, while simultaneously throwing and catching baby dolls. This was in no way an 'authentic' performance, but it was physically impressive, visually striking and utterly hilarious – a triumph of comic choreography.[9] After the choral interludes the audience laughed out loud conspicuously more than before, even though their response to the non-musical scenes was generally more muted and uncertain. This is worth noting, because (as we have already observed a number of times) Menander is not always straightforwardly funny: the mood can often shift disconcertingly from moment to moment.[10] One important function of the chorus – if the director chooses to use it in this way – can be to remind the audience that this play is a comedy, even if what takes place on stage often evokes a mixed response more complex than laughter.

*

[II.1: *Demeas and Moschion*] *Fragments survive of a scene of dialogue between father and son. Moschion persuades Demeas not to be angry with Chrysis; the topic changes to that of the forthcoming marriage of Moschion and Plangon (119–62).*

Chrysis' status and the fragility of human relationships

When Moschion asks Demeas why he is looking so grim, his father responds: 'Why? Because it seems that the courtesan that I've had in my house is actually my wife, quite unbeknowst to me' (129–31). The precise form of words is important because it reflects just how ambiguous or paradoxical Chrysis' situation appears: she cannot simultaneously be married (*gametē*) and a courtesan (*hetaira*). Technically, in fact, she is neither. A better word to describe her would be *pallakē* – 'concubine' or 'mistress'. This term denotes a woman (free or slave) in a lasting, non-commercial relationship with a man who would theoretically be free to marry.[11] Demeas cannot marry Chrysis because she is a non-Athenian, but she is a permanent (or at least long-term) member of his household and behaves more or less like a wife: she runs the house, organizes social events there, hobnobs on equal terms with the respectable women next door, and generally believes that her relationship with Demeas is a loving and stable one.[12]

But is her situation really so stable? Menander has already taken care to inform us (24–6) that not so very long ago Chrysis was a prostitute, with several paying customers vying for her favours. A little later in the play (377–9) we will see Demeas reminding Chrysis that she used to be poor before he took her in, and telling her that she will have to return to a rackety life of prostitution and poverty if he throws her out (391–7):

> Back in the city you'll see yourself very clearly for what you are! Women of your sort, Chrysis, tarts [*hetairai*] who charge a mere ten drachmas for their services, go running off to dinner parties, and they drink themselves to death on neat wine – or they go hungry, unless they get down to the job quickly and willingly … Oh, but I was forgetting, no one knows this better than you.

It is obvious that this relationship can very quickly turn sour, and it is somewhat shocking to discover how cruel Demeas can be towards his mistress. We don't see this till Act III (at which point Demeas is livid because he believes, wrongly, that Chrysis has cuckolded him with his own son). But it is worth mentioning here because it illustrates how Chrysis' status could change at any moment. As David Konstan observes, 'it is sobering to reflect how thin the line is between *pallakē* and *hetaira*, depending more on the grace of the male who takes her in than on a hard and fast distinction between roles.'[13]

In this respect it is important to note that the words used by other characters to describe Chrysis, throughout the play, are inconsistent. Here at the start of Act II Demeas calls her a 'courtesan-wife' (*gametē hetaira*); elsewhere she is referred to variously as a *pallakē* ('mistress' or 'concubine', 508), *gunē* ('woman' or 'wife', 561) or *hetaira* ('courtesan', 21, 21, 393). At the height of his anger Demeas even uses the word *chamaitupē* ('whore', 348), an insulting slang term for the lowest sort of prostitute (it literally means 'one who bangs her clients on the floor').[14] This recurrent verbal ambiguity underlines Chrysis' precarious position in the household, but it also seems designed to make the audience question her real identity and nature. 'You'll see yourself very clearly for what you are,' Demeas spitefully tells her (391). But what *is* she, in truth? As we have already seen, Chrysis does not conform to the stereotypical 'comic courtesan' figure (even though her mask identifies her as such), but this means that she is genuinely difficult to pin down.[15] Each successive scene challenges our understanding of the sort of character Chrysis is.

Nonetheless, we need to ask whether Chrysis' status is really any more doubtful than that of any of the other characters. If we look closely at any of the relationships in *Samia,* it soon becomes obvious that they are all extremely fragile. As we shall see, the loving bond between father and adopted son is loosened through fear and mutual misunderstanding; the long-established friendship between the two old men quickly turns into mistrust and violent enmity; suspicion not only undermines Nikeratos' relationship with his own wife and daughter but even leads him to the brink of committing murder.[16] Just the smallest catalyst, often arising from a simple misapprehension, can cause any relationship to implode in an instant. No one is safe. Menander's social world is one in which apparently functional relationships are perpetually poised on the brink of collapse, and beneath which deep anxieties lurk. Social status, identity, financial security, respectability, love, friendship, family ties: all of these aspects of life are under threat.

What we see in Menander's plays time after time – not just in *Samia* – might be described as 'the eruption of fear and hatred into the relationships of everyday social life'. This quotation is not in fact a description of Menander's comedy: it comes from 'Regulated Hatred', D.W. Harding's classic study of the world created by Jane Austen. Harding demonstrates how Austen's novels, despite their surface appearance of 'comforting, urbane, escapist fiction', embody a much more critical and ironical view of life. He argues that Austen's underlying concern lies in the disparity between appearances and reality, and the tensions and fissures that disrupt the ostensibly civilized social order.[17] It seems to me that this description applies remarkably well (*mutandis mutatis*) to Menander, and that 'regulated hatred' might indeed be an apt way of summing up his characters' interactions with one another. Whether we find it all amusing or profoundly unsettling is a matter of personal taste.

Comic morality and quotable quotes

When Demeas angrily announces that he has no intention of bringing up a bastard son, Moschion, his legitimate son, tries to change his mind by questioning whether there is any genuine difference between a legitimate and an illegitimate person (134–8). His motivation is perfectly clear to the audience – Moschion simply wants to prevent his son from being cast out of the house, and prefers to use slippery rhetoric than to admit the truth – but his choice of argument is a surprising one. As Daniel Ogden has pointed out, the idea that bastardy is essentially a social construct rather than a natural state is the sort of paradox that one finds in Euripidean tragedy. It might sound like a provocative challenge to conventional morality, but it seems unlikely that Menander's audience were supposed to take it very seriously, given the paramount importance of legitimate offspring both here and in all his other comic plots.[18] Certainly Demeas treats the idea as a joke ('Are you kidding?' he replies at 139), but Moschion responds by recasting the concept in the form of a moralizing maxim (140–3):

> Birth, as I see it, makes no difference. No, if one examines the matter honestly, the decent person is legitimate, while the wicked person is both illegitimate and servile.

This is the first of several maxims (*gnōmai*) that appear in the play.[19] In antiquity Menander was famous for filling his plays with quotable maxims of this sort, concerning themes such as love, friendship, parenthood, wealth and poverty, or the vicissitudes of fortune. Such passages tend to be memorable and neatly self-contained, filling one, two or three lines of verse. They almost seem deliberately designed to be excerpted from their context and cited as free-standing statements of universal wisdom or general advice for life.[20] Many readers in antiquity did indeed excerpt these portions and preserved them in the form of anthologies of quotations. Collections of Menander's maxims – the so-called *Menandrou Monostichoi* or *Menandrou Gnōmai* – remained in circulation throughout antiquity and much later, and until the papyrus rediscoveries in the twentieth century they represented our main source of knowledge of Menander's work.[21] (In fact, Moschion's lines here were known – as 'Menander fragment 248' – long before the rediscovery of *Samia*, because they were preserved by Stobaeus, an anthologist of the fifth century CE.) Over the years these anthologies grew in size, accumulating a lot of spurious material that is demonstrably not by Menander. So strongly did the playwright come to be associated with the quotable quote as a medium of expression that almost *any* moralizing soundbite, it seems, could be regarded as a 'Menandrean' maxim.

Now that it is once again possible to read entire plays by Menander, two important observations can be made about his deployment of maxims. First of all, there are far fewer maxims in these plays, line for line, than one might have expected. Secondly, the way in which these gnomic verses function within their original context can often make them seem more complex, or funnier, or more ironical, than when they are read out of context. Factors such as their position or timing within the plot, or the identity and status of the speaker, need to be taken into account.[22] Typically these lofty, moralizing statements sound much less confident or trustworthy when they are uttered by characters who are visibly confused and mistaken about everything around them. Frequently they are found in the mouth of the wrong sort of speaker – as in the example above, which would sound more authoritative if uttered by an older or wiser character, but coming from the feeble and immature Moschion just sounds pompous and unconvincing.[23] Furthermore, when we compare and contrast different works we can see that Menander's use of maxims is not consistent but varies considerably from play to play. Sometimes, as in *Dyskolos*, the maxims are apparently serious and earnest, while in *Epitrepontes*, by contrast, every single maxim seems to be undermined, destabilized or made ridiculous by the context or choice of speaker.

In general, as David Bain has observed of Menander's supposed moralizing purpose, 'this was a case easier to sustain when all we had of him was fragmentary quotation'.[24] It is clear that the image of Menander as gnomologist *par excellence* was largely a product of later processes of reception.[25] It was readers and scholars long after the playwright's death who fragmented his works and transformed them into books of quotable quotes. But Menander's contemporaries would have interpreted these maxims primarily as part of a performance. There are big differences between these two modes of reading in terms of their payoff for the audience. Menander *qua* gnomologist comes across as a profound (or even somewhat po-faced) moralist, a source of sober ethical instruction; but Menander *qua* writer for the stage seems more interested in entertaining us and making us laugh. I tend to prefer the latter version; but that is not to deny Menander any sort of serious moral purpose. Even if he is seen as playing around with *gnōmai*, we might decide that he has an implicit point to make. Perhaps he is trying to make us see that morality depends on specific situations rather than universal precepts, or to make us question for ourselves whether the meaning of life can really be packaged up so neatly as a collection of soundbites. (There are various other ways, too, in which Menander can be seen as engaging with serious philosophical ideas, as we shall see in the next section.)

The power of happenstance

When Moschion has left the stage to get ready for the forthcoming nuptials, Demeas delivers a monologue which begins with another quotable maxim (163–4):

> Happenstance [*to automaton*] is somehow a kind of god, so it seems!
> It takes care of everything that is hidden from our sight.

This two-line motto, which for many centuries was known only as 'Menander fragment 249', was excerpted by the anthologer Stobaeus and included among a lot of other proverbial wisdom relating to 'the unpredictability of life'. In their original context in this scene the lines come across as an expression of astonishment rather than a proverbial statement of truth: this is shown by the diffident and uncertain tone ('somehow . . . so it seems'). Demeas is amazed that Moschion, whom he thought would need to be persuaded to marry Plangon, turned out to be in love with her all along (165–6). He is so surprised by this coincidence that he cannot make sense of it except by assuming that happenstance must actually be a supernatural power at work behind the scenes. This might strike us as a somewhat exaggerated or naive reaction to events, but it needs to be seen in a wider context: it is not just an idiosyncrasy of Demeas or a one-off joke.

In fact this is only one of many passages in fourth-century comedy where characters use the idea of happenstance or fortune (*to automaton*, *tychē* and similar expressions in Greek) as a way of making sense of the bewildering events taking place around them.[26] The concept is inherently ambiguous, since – like the word 'fortune' in English – it can denote either cause or effect. Additionally, if it is treated as a cause, it might be seen either as an abstract power at work in the cosmos or as a personified deity. All of these different senses are encountered throughout Menander's work. For example, happenstance might be held responsible for rapid changes of fortune (*Dyskolos* 271–87; *Georgos* fr. 2); or seen as intervening to correct human mistakes (*Epitrepontes* 1108); or appealed to by characters for help in adversity (*Aspis* 213–5); or described as training people like gymnasts to cope better with their circumstances (fr. 89); or said to be working to frustrate humans' deliberate efforts (fr. 67); or even placed on the stage in person as a divine prologue-speaker, presiding over the whole plot (*Aspis* 97–148). Happenstance is mentioned in *Samia* less than in other plays, but it is invoked again by Demeas, in Act III, as an explanation for a crucial turn in the plot (that is, how he accidentally came to overhear a conversation about the baby's parentage and drew the wrong conclusion: 228–36, 259). It also features in the prologue (55), where Moschion (in an obscure and damaged passage) mentions *to automaton* as a factor involved in Chrysis' arrival in the household.[27] In all such passages an implicit or explicit contrast is being made between different causal factors. How far do humans possess independent responsibility to guide their own affairs, and how far are they acting under the influence of forces outside their control?

These are weighty questions, to be sure, but one of the big problems with making sense of any of this material – as so often when we encounter big ideas in comedy – is that it is hard to know just how seriously to take any of it. It has frequently been noted that the nature of *tychē* was a subject of interest to fourth-century philosophers, including Aristotle (who discussed the operation of chance in relation to human activity in his *Nicomachean Ethics* and *Physics*), Theophrastus (who apparently privileged chance over wisdom in his work *Callisthenes, or On Grief*) and Demetrius of Phaleron (who wrote an entire treatise *On Happenstance*).[28] Since Menander was working within the same intellectual context as these writers, broadly speaking, it seems a reasonable assumption that traces of their ideas can be found in his plays, in one form or another. Clearly there are connections to be made between Menander and contemporary thought, not just concerning *tychē* but also relating to Peripatetic ideas about character and ethics more generally: Theophrastus' *Characters*, in particular, has often been linked to Menander's use of stereotypical character types.[29] This does not necessarily mean that Menander was seriously engaging with philosophy. Perhaps, like Aristophanes before him, he was merely flirting with fashionable ideas that were in the air, or peppering his plays with a few superficial references and allusions, or even making fun of the intellectuals. But alternatively, if we choose to do so, we can read Menander's plays as serious expositions of philosophical ideas through the medium of drama.

Valeria Cinaglia's recent book *Aristotle and Menander on the Ethics of Understanding* is a good example of this latter approach: it represents a sustained attempt to treat Menander 'philosophically' in the light of Aristotelian concepts of ethical agency.[30] Even though (as Cinaglia concedes) no specific signs of influence can be detected, it is possible to regard both Aristotle and Menander as inhabiting the same 'thought world' and sharing the same sort of intellectual framework in which to make sense of ethical problems. According to Cinaglia, Menander has something genuinely serious to say about the role of happenstance in human relationships: 'For both Aristotle and Menander, chance events and cases of accidental ignorance turn out to be indispensable ingredients of the human condition because they challenge human rationality and are significant elements in the evaluation of an agent's intentions and choices.'[31]

In a series of careful and compelling close readings, Cinaglia shows that Menander's comedies can be read as a working-out of Aristotelian theories. But is this how he intended his plays to be read? There is some room for doubt. One potential problem with this sort of approach is that it could be applied to just about any dramatic or literary work in which human error and misunderstanding play a part. Aristophanes, Feydeau, Shakespeare, Oscar Wilde, Gilbert and Sullivan, P.G. Wodehouse, A.A. Milne – all of these writers (for example) could be subjected to analysis according to an Aristotelian framework, and perhaps Aristotle could help us to reach a more nuanced understanding of the ethical aspects of their works, but that is not to say that those works were deliberately designed to show philosophical principles at work. An additional and more serious problem, in my view, is that Cinaglia doesn't allow a big enough role for humour in the general scheme of things (it is telling that the words 'humour' and 'funny' do not appear anywhere in her book).

Individual readers are at liberty, of course, to read Menander as seriously or as frivolously as they like. But at any rate there are other ways of approaching the topic of happenstance in *Samia* and other comedies. One way would be to see all these references as a form of self-conscious metatheatrical commentary. By emphasizing the importance of improbable coincidences and the apparent lack of design behind the events of the plot, perhaps Menander is implicitly drawing attention to his own role as author: everyone knows that it is really the playwright who has the god-like power to decide what happens next. (This sort of reading particularly suits the quasi-authorial prologue of Tyche in Menander's *Aspis*, but it has a potentially much wider application.) Another way would be to examine the relationship between drama and Athenian popular theology: we might try to relate the sort of things Menander's characters say about *tychē* to what they say about the gods and religious ritual in general, or we might suspect some more specific sort of reference to the (fairly recently established) Athenian cult of the goddess Tyche.[32] Yet another line of approach might involve looking at the relationship between comedy and tragedy. *Tychē* features prominently in the metaphysical scheme of fifth-century tragedy, and it is especially associated with the works of Euripides.[33] Introducing this theme into his plays could be seen as one among a number of ways in which Menander deliberately evokes the world of tragedy.[34] When his characters invoke happenstance as a cause, or complain about the apparent randomness and uncertainty of life, their outbursts often sound distinctly 'tragic' – which might be either a way of adding genuine pathos or, more commonly, a way of generating further amusement by means of parody.

Are we to interpret Demeas' words (and similar utterances) as ironical jokes arising from the characters' confusion, as profound metaphysical or ethical speculations, as expressions of real-life religious practice, as metatheatrical nods to the power of the author, as examples of paratragic pastiche – or as all of the above? Probably there are several different layers of meaning at work simultaneously: there is no reason to think that these interpretations are mutually exclusive. But it is important to keep in mind that these are not extracts from a philosophical book or a lecture in the Academy; they are lines in a comedy, delivered before a theatre audience. This means (I assume) that Menander, even if he does have a serious intellectual purpose, is primarily aiming to entertain us and make us laugh. We should always be on the lookout for humour if we want to understand how these plays work. Their complex, nuanced effect depends on the precise mixture of seriousness and silliness.

*

[II.2: *Demeas, Nikeratos, Parmenon*] *Fragments of a conversation in which Demeas gets Nikeratos to agree to hold the wedding this very day. The slave Parmenon is told to fetch provisions and hire a cook; Nikeratos goes into his house to give instructions to his wife (167–205).*

In and out of the house

This short scene is extremely busy in terms of the three characters' movements. Demeas seems to be on stage constantly, though he moves between the doorways of both houses and calls out to those inside; meanwhile Parmenon bustles in and out of his master's house, and Nikeratos repeatedly goes in and out of his own house.

All of these entrances and exits have the effect of concentrating our attention on the stage building and, in particular, on the two doorways. It is worth pausing for a moment to consider exactly what we see as we sit looking down at the stage. The visual style of classical Greek theatre might be described as minimalist. In a big outdoor theatre, there is little possibility of creating a 'theatrical illusion' in the sense of a realistic stage set or scenery.[35] We simply have to accept, for the duration of the performance, that what we can see in front of us – a large, flat acting space (*orchēstra*) with a stage building (*skēnē*) to its rear and an altar somewhere in the middle – represents an Athenian street scene. (In other plays exactly the same performance space, with minimal alteration, would have had to stand for many other fictional locations.) The stage building has several doorways, two of which are used here to represent the front doors of Demeas' and Nikeratos' houses. No doubt it would be possible to add some sort of painted backdrop or other decoration to the stage building, suggesting architectural or topographic detail, but there is no way of knowing whether any such decoration was used here.[36] Beside Demeas' doorway is a household shrine of Apollo *Aguieus*, presumably with a visible bust or pillar representing the god: when Demeas passes it at line 444 he calls out a greeting.

To stage left and stage right there are two gangways (*eisodoi* or *parodoi*), and we have to imagine that these represent two different destinations. One of them is imagined as leading to the countryside, and the other as leading to the city and harbour. When actors make their entrances and exits, they have to do so using one of the gangways or one of the doors. In each case, a principle of contrast and symmetry is clearly marked on a visual level. In this scene the entrances and exits can be mapped out as follows:[37]

Door 1 (Demeas)	***Door 2 (Nikeratos)***	***Gangway 1 (towards city)***
	(167) Demeas shouts to Nikeratos indoors; Nikeratos emerges from the house	
(189–90) Demeas calls to Parmenon inside his own house; Parmenon emerges		
(195) Parmenon goes back inside Demeas' house to get money		
	(198a) Nikeratos goes inside to talk to his wife	
(198b) Parmenon emerges from house with basket		
		(198–202) Parmenon exits stage gradually in direction of city
	(203–4) Nikeratos emerges, complaining about his wife	
(205–) Demeas goes indoors		(205–) Nikeratos exits, following Parmenon to city

What we can't see, of course, is what goes on inside the two houses, even though this is a major source of interest. In reality the interior of the stage building may just be an actors' dressing room. But conceptually and thematically these unseen domestic interiors are extremely important. One could say that Menander's plays are all about what happens behind closed doors – private conversations, intrigues, intimate relationships and embarrassing family secrets. For the duration of the plot, the houses' doors are thrown open, and their secrets spill out into the public domain. The way in which the *skēnē* doors are used, in *Samia* and elsewhere, shows that even when they are open it is impossible for the spectators to see inside the building. But by recurrently drawing our attention to the two doorways – with frequent entrances and exits, scenes of door-knocking and door-opening, unrealistically loud noises of creaking bolts and so on – Menander obviously wants to tantalize us and arouse our curiosity.[38]

In this respect, it is instructive to point out one crucial difference between the Greek theatre and other types of *mise-en-scène*. In most modern theatrical productions, films and television shows, the audience can actually see the fictional domestic interiors. All the action conventionally takes place indoors but in full view, because the stage or film set represents the rooms of the characters' houses or apartments. In ancient comedy and tragedy, by contrast, the interior scenes are almost completely invisible. Either the action takes place outside in the street, an important way in which these plays flout strict realism, or it must be described through narrative rather than acted out directly in front of us. There is a huge difference between what we see and what we are induced to imagine – or, to put it in more theoretical terms, between *mimetic space* (what is represented on stage) and *diegetic space* (what is communicated only verbally).[39] In Menander's world, both categories of space are important for understanding the play's meaning.

'Her Indoors'

The invisible domestic interior is significant in another way: it is the space in which the female characters mostly live out their lives, and the main (or only) sphere in which women are able to exert power and influence. In comedy just as in everyday Athenian life, respectable women usually remained indoors.

One such woman is Nikeratos' wife. She never speaks a single line, and never even appears (unless we are to assume that she comes on stage, as a mute 'extra', for the wedding scene at the very end of the play). Nevertheless, she is, in a way, the funniest character in *Samia*. The fact that she never emerges outside the house might be thought to add verisimilitude to the social setting depicted in the play, but probably the main explanation for her non-appearance is that it is simply more amusing to present her as an off-stage presence. This allows Nikeratos and the other characters to build up an image of her as a purely monstrous comic grotesque. Mrs Nikeratos can be seen as an early example of a familiar stock figure – the wife-as-ogre. The character type has a long afterlife, stretching far beyond the genre of ancient comedy. It will be familiar to modern readers from a hundred and one variety shows, sitcoms and stand-up routines (and if it isn't, a quick session with Google and YouTube will soon put you in the picture). Across different time periods and cultures one can identify a certain variety of male comedian who delights in depicting his wife as a vexatious harridan. Such a wife is not very clearly individualized or named: she might be referred to as 'the wife', 'the missus', 'Her Indoors', 'She Who Must Be Obeyed', 'the old ball-and-chain', or similar. In fact the wife-as-ogre, rather like her close relation, the comic mother-in-law, is not a real person so much as a fictional construct. The entire *raison d'être* of the character is simply to be the butt of misogynistic jokes. So it is with Mrs Nikeratos – who, we now note, is not given a name. The reason for her anonymity is much the same as the reason why she doesn't appear on stage: she isn't really a character at all, just an imaginary figure of fun.

Just look at the sort of thing that Nikeratos and the other men in the play say about 'Her Indoors'. In this scene (197–9) Nikeratos vanishes inside the house to give her instructions about the wedding preparations, but as soon as he has left the stage, Demeas turns to the audience and says, in a confidential aside: 'Persuading his wife is going to cause him a load of trouble!' (200–1). In other words, the spectators must infer that Her Indoors is already well known for obstructing her husband's plans and being disagreeable, and they are being primed to view her in an unsympathetic light. (Are all the spectators men, I wonder?[40]) But they have already been given a small hint that Mrs Nikeratos is a formidable figure: we may perhaps recall Moschion shuddering when she was mentioned by Parmenon in Act I (69).

It comes as no surprise, then, that the tête-à-tête between husband and wife does not go well. It certainly doesn't take very long, since

Nikeratos emerges from the house again just five lines later – that is, after a gap of maybe thirty seconds. In comedy we can never be sure whether a character's absence from the stage plays out in 'real time', but this does seem to have been a remarkably short, sharp exchange. When Nikeratos comes out of the doorway he is complaining about his wife's behaviour (203–5). The text is badly damaged at this point, but if we accept the supplements and conjectures printed in Arnott's edition, it seems that Nikeratos is describing their exchange using words such as *periergos* ('nosy' or 'interfering') or *hēlikon lalei* ('how greatly she is prattling away').[41]

At the beginning of Act IV, Nikeratos emerges from his house onto the stage mid-conversation with Her Indoors, using the convention known as 'talking back'.[42] This technique, which is very common in Menander, is designed to give the impression that there really is a house (not a dressing room) on the other side of the door: it is the closest approximation to interior scenes that we encounter on the comic stage. All that we hear Nikeratos saying is: '... you'll wear me out, woman!' (421), but this (as it were) overheard snatch of dialogue shows that their conversation took the form of a heated argument. The same technique, and the same argumentative tone, is used in Act V, where Nikeratos comes out of the house shouting: '... don't be so irritating!' (713). We are not privy to any further verbal exchanges of this sort, but there is one memorable moment when things turn really nasty. In the middle of Act IV, Nikeratos is so angry with Her Indoors that he decides to kill her, although he is narrowly prevented from doing so by Demeas (580–3). Would he really have committed uxoricide? Almost certainly not. As with all threats of fatality in the world of comedy, it does not cause real alarm because we know it cannot happen.[43] So we must assume that it is just funny to imagine the ogre-wife getting her comeuppance at last.

It hardly needs saying that this, the only stable domestic relationship in the play, stands as a terrible sort of advertisement for married bliss. Is Menander implying that this is the sort of life that Moschion and Plangon have to look forward to in future? Perhaps so. The marriage of

Nikeratos and Her Indoors is not uniquely dysfunctional – far from it. Indeed, every long-established marriage in comedy appears to be more or less the same. If we look at other Greek and Roman comedies, we find a whole array of wives-as-ogres. There are a few variations on the character type. Sometimes these wives might be given a name or a more clearly delineated character, or sometimes they might emerge from the house to play a more active role in the plot (the unnamed wife in Plautus' *Menaechmi* and Cleostrata in *Casina* stand out particularly in this respect). Even when wives are not really ogre-like, their husbands still treat them as if they were (see, for example, Laches' treatment of his wife in Terence's *Self-Tormentor*, or Chremes' scenes with his wife in *The Mother-In-Law*; Charisios' marriage to Pamphile in Menander's *Epitrepontes* initially falls into this category, though it turns out to be a more complex case). In almost every comedy married couples are depicted as unhappy or ill-matched.[44] Furthermore, the awfulness of wives was among the most popular themes for quotable maxims in comedy.[45] Time after time it is taken for granted that husbands and wives will naturally be at odds with one another. We can try to account for this tendency in various ways – clearly it is meant to be humorous; clearly it functions as a running joke or cliché; clearly it is not a completely realistic portrayal of married life; clearly no one should be surprised by the presence of a strong vein of misogyny in ancient Greek culture. But what is not so clear is exactly why this view of marriage is so prevalent, or exactly why it is meant to be funny. Given that the pursuit of marriage is essentially the main driving force behind all these comic plots, it seems paradoxical that married life should be presented in such a dismal light.

3

Third Act

[III.1: *Demeas alone*] *A little time has passed. In a monologue to the audience Demeas relates how he accidentally overheard a conversation between the female servants, and later happened to see Chrysis nursing the baby. On this basis he has concluded – mistakenly, as the audience knows – that Moschion and Chrysis are the parents of the child. He is greatly perturbed (206–82).*

Show versus tell

Everything that Demeas tells us here is imagined as having taken place in private, behind the closed doors of his house. If the conventions of the Greek theatre allowed the staging of interior scenes, it is easy to imagine how these events could have been acted out. The image of Demeas hiding in the pantry and eavesdropping, or catching a glimpse of Chrysis suckling the baby while he remained out of sight, or reacting with exaggerated shock and horror – all of this could have been staged in a vivid and visually exciting way. But Menander, here as often elsewhere, uses a monologue to convey these important plot developments.[1] This decision was not simply dictated by convention. Actually there is nothing about these events that necessitates their taking place inside. If he had wanted to do so, Menander could have set the scene out of doors. Numerous scenes from other Greek and Roman comedies, involving eavesdropping, concealment, selective visibility/invisibility, or the use of supposedly inaudible 'asides', suggest ways in which this might have been managed.[2] (Note that at the end of this monologue, for instance, Demeas remains on stage, apparently unseen by the other characters who enter.) So why does Menander choose to tell us things rather than show us? And why is this monologue so very long? This is meant to be drama, after all. Might it not seem that the use of narrative rather than action is decidedly undramatic – even (dare one think it) rather boring?

Unless we assume that Menander was dramaturgically incompetent, we must look for positive reasons why monologues might sometimes be preferred to staged action. One explanation is that they are a means of providing variety, contrast and changes of pace within a play's structure. Another explanation is that long monologues are not necessarily dull. No doubt many of Menander's audience members enjoyed listening to them, just as they evidently enjoyed law-court speeches or other forms of rhetorical display (*epideixis*): we must beware of judging ancient drama by modern tastes. Menander is not the only ancient dramatist to make frequent use of narrative within drama: the Greek tragedians were also well known for their set-piece monologues, messenger-speeches, prologue-speeches and rhetorical debates (*agōnes*), and it is clear that these scenes were often treated as the plays' highlights rather than the boring bits in between the action.[3] Menander's penchant for monologues represents just one among several ways in which his comedies resemble tragedies (an aspect of his work which I discuss elsewhere).[4]

Another explanation is that even though the monologue might strike us as a static and restrictive mode of performance, it actually offers considerable scope for an actor to demonstrate his versatility. Impersonation and role-switching are often involved, as here in this scene, since the narrator is often required to report the words of other characters verbatim.[5] In the course of performing this particular monologue, the actor playing Demeas has to mimic the voices and mannerisms of several others – the hubbub of a group of female servants at work in the kitchen (226–7), the cooing baby-talk of an elderly nurse (242–8), and a dialogue between the nurse and a housemaid (251–9) – as well as maintaining his own role as a man in the grip of confusion and jealous rage. If done skilfully, this could be very effective in the theatre.

The use of monologues can have an additional advantage in a play such as *Samia* or other 'comedies of misunderstanding'. The first-person narrative format enables the speaker to describe their own thought processes explicitly and in some detail. This makes it much easier for us to follow these thought processes than if we were merely to watch the characters getting confused and making mistakes. In this scene, Demeas takes us step-by-step through his reactions to the events as they unfolded: what is particularly striking is the frequency of words relating to sensory perception (213–14, 264, 265, 271, 277) and cognitive function or reasoning (216, 217–18, 225, 240, 265, 267, 270, 272, 275, 277, 279).

Demeas begins by mixing a couple of well-worn metaphors – a storm at sea and an unanticipated knock-out blow in boxing – to emphasize the suddenness of the shock that he has experienced and its physical impact on him (206–9, 215). He says that he has come to doubt the evidence of his own eyes (213–14), and he turns to the audience and asks them to decide: 'Is this credible? Consider for yourselves whether I'm in my right mind or whether I'm mad' (216–17). He goes on to give us a detailed description of the interior layout of his house in order to explain exactly how he came to overhear the crucial conversation about the baby's paternity (225–48):

> The baby had been chucked down on a couch out of the way and was howling. The women kept shouting 'Flour! Water! Oil! Coal!' all at the same time. I myself went to fetch one or other of these things and take it to them. I happened to go into the pantry, and I did not come out straight away because I was taking my time looking for something and taking out more supplies. At the same time as I was doing all that, a woman came down from the upper storey and went into the room that was directly in front of the storeroom – that room happens to be a weaving room, built in such a way that one has to pass through it in order to go upstairs or go to the pantry. The woman was the nurse of Moschion, a rather elderly person, and nowadays free, though she used to be a slave of mine. When she saw the child crying and unattended, she went up to him. Since she didn't know I was in the

> room to hear her, she thought that she could talk to him freely. She went up and spoke to him, saying the sort of thing that people say – 'Dearest little one', and 'my great treasure', and 'where's Mummy?' – and she gave him a kiss and carried him about. When he had stopped crying, she said to herself: 'Dear me, it seems only the other day that I was nursing Moschion himself! I took care of him just the same as you, but now he has a little boy of his own . . .'

A little later Demeas describes his reaction to seeing Chrysis with the baby at her breast, and his jumping immediately to the wrong conclusion. 'It's a known fact [*gnōrimon*] that she is the baby's mother,' he announces (267) – though of course we know better. It seems that the impact of this new 'knowledge' has thrown Demeas into confusion and self-contradiction. Even though he has just heard Moschion being named as the baby's father, he cannot bring himself to accept the fact, and he now expresses doubt. He wonders whether he himself or someone else might be the father, and he becomes incoherent, breaking off in the middle of a phrase to appeal to the audience: 'No, I do not say this to you, gentlemen . . . I have no suspicion . . . but I bring the facts of the matter out into the open, along with what I have heard' (269–71). Finally, just before he is interrupted by the reappearance of Parmenon, Demeas explains that different processes of reasoning have led him to contradictory conclusions. On the basis of his intimate knowledge of Moschion's character, he reasons that Moschion cannot possibly have treated his adoptive father so disrespectfully (272–4); but then again, on the basis that the nurse did not realize she was being overheard, he reasons that what she said must have been the truth (275–9). What is he to think?

As a study in character and psychology this speech is full of interest. It has also been discussed in relation to the question of comedy's engagement with contemporary philosophy (see pp. 48–55), since Menander's dramatization of the process of making mistakes can be seen as sharing certain features with Aristotelian concepts of *hamartia* (human error) and *anagnōrisis* ('recognition', defined as the transition from ignorance to knowledge).[6] At the same time, Demeas' speech also evokes a legal setting. It has been pointed out that Demeas addresses the spectators as if they were jurors in a law court, in much the same manner as Moschion did at the start of Act I. The use of direct address to the audience; the narrative of the alleged facts in the case; the detailed description of the *locus in quo* (the 'place at which' the cause of action occurred); the emphasis on evidence and types of proof; the quoting of other people's words as witness statements; the use of rhetorical tropes such as the argument from probability (225) and the argument from character (272–4); the invitation to the spectators to judge the case for themselves – all these features of the monologue are strongly reminiscent of forensic oratory.[7] As Christopher Carey puts it, this speech is 'one of Menander's cleverest examples of code-switching to create a meta-fictive context'.[8] In other words, Demeas' monologue shifts between two different fictional worlds: the normally self-contained setting of the play, in which the spectators merely watch from the outside, and an imaginary quasi-law court, in which their presence is explicitly acknowledged and they are (in effect) invited to assume the role of jury members.

Far from being boring, this monologue is a fascinating and multi-layered scene, with plenty of potential for entertainment. It not only contributes significantly to our understanding of the plot and characters but also draws us into the action as virtual participants.

By the end of his long speech Demeas has worked himself up into a state of considerable agitation ('I'm completely beside myself!' 279), but before he can say or do anything else the scene is brought abruptly to an end by the return of Parmenon, who is not alone. Demeas remains on stage, but the newcomers are deep in conversation and do not notice him. Thus the frame shifts back to the normal setting of the play, the virtual courtroom dissolves (as it were) into thin air, the spectators resume their passive role as onlookers, and the plot continues to move forward.

*

[III.2: *Demeas, Parmenon, the cook, attendant(s)*] *Parmenon returns from the market, accompanied by a cook and laden with provisions for the wedding feast (283–95).*

A rare joke

As I am at pains to demonstrate throughout this book, Menander can be very amusing. But the very fact that this requires demonstration is telling. (Shouldn't it be obvious?) 'They are pleasantly written, these plays,' it has been said, 'but . . . at their worst they are very dull indeed. They are not funny.'[9] Is this a fair assessment? Whether or not one laughs at any particular moment is a matter of personal temperament to a large extent. It is also important to keep reminding ourselves that what might have seemed funny (to someone or other) *circa* 300 BCE will not necessarily seem funny today. Nevertheless, even Menander's most enthusiastic fans are forced to admit that his sense of humour is, let us say, somewhat oblique. W.G. Arnott's useful descriptive survey of the subject begins by acknowledging that humour in Menander 'is clearly less abundant' than elsewhere in ancient comedy, and concedes that Menander's audience probably smiled more often than they laughed out loud.[10] Stephen Halliwell, in a wide-ranging discussion of laughter in Greek culture, argues that the distinctive quality of Menander's comedy depends on the *intermittent* presence or absence of laughter. This fluctuation is compared to the artistic technique of chiaroscuro, and it marks a complete difference from Aristophanes, whose comedy is more consistently and continually funny.[11]

One can try to defend or explain Menander from various angles, but it seems likely that the main reason why people don't tend to find Menander immediately funny is that he very seldom uses verbal humour. It is difficult to find examples of jokes, wordplay, puns or other witticisms in his comedies. (For this reason, Menander suffers less from being read in the medium of translation than any other classical dramatist – which may perhaps be seen as an incidental compensation for the shortage of big laughs.) The verbal texture of the dialogue, although it does contain variations in colour and register, seems flat; the content is often banal; the vocabulary is relatively limited and ordinary; there is no obvious exuberance or sparkle on a linguistic level.[12] If verbal humour is what we expect from our comedians, then inevitably we will prefer Aristophanes or Plautus. What Menander gives us is a more subtle, restrained type of humour, arising largely from character, situational irony and incongruity. It is an acquired taste, to be sure.

All of this means that when we do come across a genuine joke in Menander we greet it as a rare and surprising phenomenon. Such flashes of verbal wit are bound to stand out because of their scarcity value, but sometimes Menander gives them extra emphasis by their position and timing within a scene. Here the very first words spoken by Parmenon, when he bursts onto the scene unannounced, are a joke (283–5):

> Gods above, cook! I don't know why you're carrying knives around with you, because your tongue is quite sharp enough to do all the chopping-up!

Boom! Boom! The humour, such as it is, depends on the fact that the Greek verb *katakoptō* has two meanings ('to chop up' and 'to be really annoying'). It's an abysmal joke, and it's not even original: the same gag appears, with minimal variations, elsewhere in comedies by Menander and others.[13] If you find yourself laughing out loud at this point, there's probably something wrong with you: a groan rather than a guffaw is called for. Perhaps we may be thinking that it's just as well that Menander doesn't really do jokes, if this lame quip is the best that he can manage.

And yet . . . could it not be that the excruciating lameness of the joke is entirely deliberate? There is an important interpretative principle at stake here. Whenever we come across a feature in Menander's work that strikes us as strange or unpleasing in some way, it is easy to criticize the playwright for ineptitude. But perhaps it is our own judgement that is at fault. It is probably better to assume that Menander did know what he was doing, and to make a special effort to understand what he was trying to achieve. Features that *prima facie* seem to be artistic blemishes or missed opportunities may on closer inspection reveal themselves to be misunderstood gems.

Why might Menander have decided to introduce this feeble 'chopping-up' wordplay? It can scarcely have escaped his notice, I think, that it is a bad joke. (Would he not have recalled the audience's groans when he used the same joke – three times! – in his *Dyskolos*?) The explanation may be that some jokes are funny precisely because they are so awful. Similarly, the joke's blatant lack of originality may be seen as a positive virtue. Good and bad jokes alike can become funnier through repetition: the comic value of 'running gags' depends on audience recognition and familiarity rather than any intrinsic qualities of the jokes themselves.[14] Sometimes, as in Aristophanes' plays, an extra level of metatheatrical humour is generated when the author self-consciously draws attention to his own use of hackneyed old gags, explicitly acknowledged as such.[15] Admittedly, there is no overt signal of metatheatricality in this case, but it may be that, by simply including the uncharacteristic joke, Menander is (in effect) saying to his audience: 'Look, I *can* do verbal humour, but do you really want it?' At any rate, the joke is hammered home relentlessly when Parmenon is made to repeat it again within the space of just a few lines (at 293–4).

At the same time, there is a simpler explanation of how the joke works, based on its comic timing and relation to the dramatic context. It is the abruptness of its obtrusion into Demeas' agitated monologue that gives the joke its particular point. It marks a complete and very sudden change of register, making it an excellent example of what Halliwell would call the 'chiaroscuro' effect.[16] Another way of describing the effect – despite the fact that it appears in a comedy! – would be 'comic relief'. If the humour had been more sophisticated, the tonal contrast would not have been quite so jarring. The joke introduces a new scene of undignified argy-bargy, with the two slave characters hurling insults at one another. Now a further explanation of the joke suggests itself: humour is closely linked to characterization. It is clear that Parmenon and the cook are exactly the sort of characters who would enjoy this sort of crude, clumsy attempt at wit.

Cooks and other minor characters

Let us pause for a moment to consider the cook. When discussing the use of recurrent character types above (pp. 14–21), I emphasized the important point that Menander likes to play around with our expectations. His young lovers, old men, courtesans, soldiers and others might look like two-dimensional 'stock characters', and they might come on stage wearing the same limited range of predictable mask types, but they tend to be much more three-dimensional than their appearance would suggest. However, the cook is an exception. All of Menander's cooks – in *Aspis*, *Dyskolos*, *Epitrepontes*, *Kolax*, *Misoumenos* and *Phasma* as well as in this play – seem to conform to type: they are precisely what we would expect. Boastful, argumentative, loquacious and slightly dishonest, the comic cook is essentially a pure stereotype. Examples of the type can be found in the remains of many comedies from the earlier part of the fourth century, and Menander seems to have inherited the character without alteration.[17] In thematic terms it is easy to see why cooks should feature so frequently in these plays, since the comic genre is noted for its preoccupation with food and drink or with domestic affairs more generally.[18] But in dramatic terms the cook always functions in more or less the same way – to provide light-hearted moments of fun and distraction from the main business of the plot.

The cook is a minor character in *Samia*, who makes only two brief appearances in Act III – here at 283–95, and a little later at 357–98 (when he continues to provide distraction by interrupting Demeas and Chrysis in the middle of a bitter quarrel). Nevertheless, at some point in antiquity, the second of his scenes was deemed sufficiently striking for it to be depicted in a commemorative artwork. A version of this image is preserved in the form of a fourth-century CE mosaic from Mytilene (discussed and illustrated later in this chapter, pp. 81–4). If the illustration can be trusted as evidence for the play's performance tradition, it gives us a plausible impression of what the cook might have looked like and what mask he wore. In the mosaic he is depicted as a black African, apparently with long dreadlocks. This unusual visual depiction is not precisely paralleled elsewhere in the archaeological record, but it corresponds in some respects to the attested mask type 26, 'the cicada' (*tettix*).[19] Pollux records that 'the *tettix* servant has a bald crown and two or three locks of black hair, and similarly a black beard, and has a cross-eyed expression'; we also have independent evidence from Athenaeus that the *tettix* mask type was used for foreign cooks.[20] Perhaps the most striking feature of this visual evidence, if we accept it as reliable, is that it reveals the cook's ethnicity. This is never mentioned in the words of the script, and there are (for instance) no jokes about foreign speech or mannerisms, but it is still a significant aspect of the character's presentation in the theatre.

Demeas, Parmenon and the cook are the only speaking characters here, but they are not the only characters on stage. It is also important to acknowledge the – to readers – almost invisible presence of one or more attendants. If the cook is a *minor* character, then these attendants are *minimal* characters. They are played by mute 'extras', who may or may not be wearing masks.[21] Their main function is to add verisimilitude and provide a sense of bustling domestic activity in the background. Perhaps they are carrying paraphernalia such as cooking pots or other culinary implements. But such minimal characters leave almost no trace in the script. Crucially, we do not even know how many there are. In fact, the only sign we have that there are any at all is that when Parmenon orders the cook to go inside he uses the plural form of the verb (*paragete*, 295), addressing cook and attendant(s) together as a group. So there must be at least one attendant present. Similar ambiguities can be seen in other places where supernumerary mute performers are used. Normally we can detect their presence only when the main characters give them instructions (which they silently carry out, one assumes).[22] Compare, for instance, the earlier moment in Act I where Demeas calls out orders to a plural group of slaves and later criticizes a single slave who is dragging his feet (104–5). Nikeratos is also on stage at this point, having just returned from travelling along with Demeas, but he gives no explicit orders. Does this mean (as some think) that Nikeratos is too poor to have any slaves to carry his luggage?

It is impossible to be certain with only the words on the page to guide us.[23] This is yet another way in which reading the script is a very different experience from watching the play in the theatre, and it is bound to make us wonder how many other 'invisible' details we are missing.

*

[III.3: *Parmenon and Demeas*] *Demeas, with threats of violence, forces Parmenon to admit that he knows who the baby's parents are. Parmenon maintains the pretence that Chrysis is the mother, but when Demeas reveals that he knows that Moschion is the father, Parmenon concedes that this is true. Thus Demeas believes that he has confirmation that his own son has cuckolded him. Demeas' rage escalates, and Parmenon flees the scene (296–325).*

Comic violence

When the cook has gone inside, Parmenon belatedly acknowledges the presence of his master, but he seems extremely cagey and reluctant to approach Demeas when summoned (294–305). Evidently he can sense that Demeas is working himself up into a dangerous state of mind. 'Now listen to me, Parmenon,' the old man now says. 'There are lots of reasons why I *don't* want to give you a good thrashing ...' (305–7). Things are looking pretty bad for Parmenon right now.

A strained exchange follows, in which Demeas rattles off a series of questions at top speed (308–24): he is so irate that he can barely wait for Parmenon to finish replying before he asks another one. Each verse is split up, with one or more changes of speaker within a single line. This style of rapid-fire dialogue (technically known as *antilabē*) is typical of Menander: it is thought to resemble naturalistic, ordinary speech, even though the formal metrical structure continues uninterrupted, and it particularly suits moments of high tension. Eventually Demeas manages to extract from Parmenon what he thinks is the truth about the baby's parentage. Since he believes that Parmenon has been either keeping secrets from him or actively conspiring to dupe him, he is enraged. First he calls to his other slaves (that is, a group of mute extras hitherto unacknowledged, as in the previous scene): 'Here! Will one of you slaves give me a leather strap to use on this scoundrel?' (321–2). When Parmenon begs him to stop, Demeas utters an even worse threat: 'I'll brand you, I swear!' (323). The terrified Parmenon runs away, with another of Demeas' slaves in pursuit (325); he will not return till Act V.

Perhaps we may think that threats of violence, like threats of suicide and murder, are neutralized when they appear in a comic setting. Characters in *Samia* often say that they are going to do awful things to one another – for example, Moschion comes close to running Nikeratos through with his sword, Demeas and Nikeratos almost come to blows, and Nikeratos at different times vows to murder his wife, set fire to the baby, or beat Chrysis with a stick – but these ferocious words are never translated into action.[24] Surely comedy is a safe zone, where nothing truly painful ever happens. By and large this is true, but there are certain exceptions to the generic rule. Cruelty to slaves is not only permissible, but is even treated as a source of humour. This uncomfortable fact, along with the plays' attitude to premarital sex, is a major impediment to a modern audience's enjoyment of ancient comedy.

Apart from Demeas' intimidating words here, there are other points in the play where slaves are threatened with violent punishment. Later in this act Demeas tells the cook: 'I'll smash your head in if you keep talking to me' (388–9); at the start of Act IV Demeas makes his household slaves weep by telling them he is going to take a cudgel to them (440–1); and in Act V Moschion says that he will give Parmenon a thrashing (662–3). The culmination of all these threats comes near the end of the play, where we move beyond words to actual bodily harm. When Parmenon tells his young master that the wedding is finally going to happen and encourages him to cheer up, Moschion all of a sudden punches him in the face (676–8). This is a shocking moment, and it throws Parmenon off balance (679–81):

Parmenon You've split my lip open!

Moschion Are you still talking?

Parmenon I'm on my way. [*aside*] By Zeus, this is an evil situation I've got myself into.

Moschion Why are you dawdling?

These lines show us that Moschion is to be imagined as actually having drawn blood. This is a real injury, and Parmenon is really in pain. Are we supposed to be laughing at his distress? Perhaps so.

Moments like this are eye-opening because of what they confirm to us about the servant–master relationship in comedy. Even though in general 'Menander portrays close and often affectionate relationships between citizens and their domestic slaves',[25] and even though in some respects Menander's slaves might seem to be cleverer or more in control than their masters, it is clear that ultimately the plays do not seriously challenge the hierarchies and norms of slave-owning society. From time to time slaves might get the better of their masters, but when we see them bleeding and weeping we are left in no doubt where the power really lies.

Menandrean insults

The Greek word that Demeas uses of Parmenon when he is about to thrash him is *asebēs* (322). In the section above I translated this as 'scoundrel'; other possible versions in English include 'blackguard' (as in Arnott's Loeb edition), 'you rogue!' (in Balme's World's Classics translation) or 'snake-in-the-grass' (in Miller's Penguin). But the literal meaning of the term is 'impious' or 'sacrilegious'. It seems an odd choice of word in the circumstances, and it raises a more general question about language use and translation.

Most of the time, as I have already observed, the language spoken by Menander's characters is ordinary and unremarkable. However, one notable exception to this tendency is their use of insults. When the characters are angry with one another (or with themselves), they resort to a surprisingly varied and exuberant range of derogatory expressions – including incongruous epithets, inaccurate descriptions, wildly exaggerated accusations of crimes committed, comparisons to famous heroes or villains of mythology, and (very occasionally) obscene or scatological language. Nothing here quite approaches the rococo zaniness of Shakespearean insults ('thou cream-faced loon', 'thou damn'd and luxurious mountain goat', and suchlike), but Menander clearly revels in the sheer joy of being rude. There is, I think, a real sense of inventiveness and comic energy here that has not been fully appreciated.

Such words pose special difficulties for translators, partly because they are almost never meant to be taken literally. Eleanor Dickey (who studies insults as a special sub-category in *Greek Forms of Address*) observes that 'the social meaning of an insult, like that of any other form of address, is not determined by its lexical meaning'; other considerations have to be taken into account, such as the high or low register of a word or the level of perceived offensiveness.[26] An additional problem is that even if we think we have understood the 'social meaning' of the insult in question, it is hard to come up with a word that bears an equivalent meaning in a different language and cultural context.

For the sake of completeness, and for the entertainment of readers whose tastes run to such things, there follows a lexicon of all the insulting words and phrases in *Samia*. In each case it is surprisingly difficult to judge the exact meaning or nuance, or the intended degree of offensiveness, so I leave the list to speak for itself. Nevertheless, it would be an instructive exercise to compare and contrast each word below with the supposedly equivalent expressions adopted in published translations.

abelteros	('silly', 126, 653)
andrapodon	('slave', 506)
androgynos	('hermaphrodite', 69)
anoētos	('mindless', 327)
apoplēktos	('victim of paralysis', 'cripple', 105)
apophtheirou	('ruin take you', 373)

asebēs	('impious', 'ungodly', 322)
authekastos	('wilful', 550)
barbaros	('barbarian', 519)
deilotatos	('most cowardly one', 654)
dusmoros	('ill-fated one', 70, 255)
exōlēs apoloio	('may you perish utterly', 367)
Helenē	('Helen of Troy', 337)
s' ho Zeus apolesai	('Zeus destroy you!' 689)
Thraix	('Thracian', 520)
idiōtēs	('amateur', 'ignoramus', 286)
hierosulos	('temple-robber', 678)
kakist' andrōn hapantōn	('most evil of all men', 492)
katharma	('garbage', 481)
katakopteis	('you chop me up', 292)
mastigias	('you who deserve a good whipping', 324)
to mega pragma	('big shot', 390)
melancholai	('he is suffering from black bile', 563)
miaros	('disgusting', 551)
nothos	('bastard', 136)
olethros	('pestilence', 'plague', 348)
periergos	('nosy', 203 [conjecturally restored], 300)
skaios	('stupid', 'clumsy', 428)
skatophagos/skatophagei	('shit-eater', 427, 550)
trachus	('rough', 550)
phluareis	('you're drivelling', 690)
chamaitupē	('prostitute who bangs her clients on the floor', 348)

*

[III.4: *Demeas alone*] *In another monologue, with overtones of tragedy, Demeas rails against the supposed misdeeds of his loved ones. He inclines to blame Chrysis more than Moschion, and he decides to throw her out of the house (325–56).*

Tragic comedy

'O citadel of the Cecropian land! O upper air, outspread! O . . . hang on, why are you shouting, Demeas? Why are you shouting, you fool? Pull yourself together!' (326–7). By opening his latest monologue with a quotation from Euripides' *Oedipus* (a play that no longer survives), Demeas gives it an unmistakably 'tragic' flavour. This is the sort of thing that Menander's characters often like to do at moments of heightened emotion or crisis.[27] In the words of Kathryn Gutzwiller (whose article 'The tragic mask of comedy' is essential reading on this topic), paratragic and metatheatrical elements in Menander 'stem from the sustained view of his characters that life is like a tragedy'.[28] By evoking a dramatic genre associated with solemnity, pity and fear, or by assimilating these comic characters to the suffering heroes of mythology, Menander might seem to be investing their situation with an extra level of pathos or profundity. But the effect created is one of irony and humour rather than genuine pathos. The spectators know that life is not really like a tragedy, and they can be sure that the plot will eventually resolve itself in comic rather than tragic mode. Thus it is perfectly clear that Demeas in this scene is wildly over-reacting. His 'tragic' behaviour – the inverted commas are crucial – is yet another sign of his general delusion.[29]

This is just one of a number of places where Menander makes use of tragic paradigms.[30] In this he is not unusual. Playing around with tragedy is something that nearly all Greek comedians like to do. They frequently resort to tragic parody, pastiche, allusion, quotation and other forms of metatheatrical reference, and they exploit the complementary contrast between the two principal dramatic genres for humorous purposes (or sometimes for more intellectual ones). This thematic preoccupation marks an important line of continuity between fifth-century and later comedy, and it has been widely discussed by scholars.[31]

Evidently Menander expected his audience to be broadly familiar with tragic as well as comic conventions. We do not necessarily need to look for a specific tragic intertext in order to make sense of the humour.

In many cases, as in this scene, it may be sufficient merely to recognize the tragic 'flavour' where it occurs (in the shape of exaggerated solemnity, over-acting, elevated diction or other easily identifiable formal features). Even if not everyone realizes that Demeas is quoting Euripides, it is obvious that he is meant to sound tragic – and that means that the basic point will be clear enough. Nevertheless, sometimes there might be an extra, more complex level of humour available for those who are able to identify specific allusions or the exact sources of quotations.

It may be that Menander had certain individual tragedies in mind, not simply the tragic genre as a whole, when he came up with the concept for the plot of *Samia*. Given the fact that Nikeratos in Act IV (498–500) explicitly compares Moschion's behaviour to that of the hero Phoenix – who was accused of seducing his father Amyntor's concubine and blinded as a punishment – it seems plausible that either Sophocles' or Euripides' *Phoenix* (both lost and surviving only in a few fragments) may have influenced Menander in some way.[32] Certainly the basic situation and plot structure are remarkably similar to that of *Samia*.[33] The theme of sexual jealousy and its potentially awful consequences, the love (real or alleged) of an older woman for a younger man, the breakdown and eventual restoration of the father–son relationship – all these elements are common to the tragic and the comic treatments. Both these tragedies are lost, though a few suggestive fragments survive. In Sophocles' version of the story mention was made of a wanton woman or prostitute (fr. 720), presumably a derogatory reference to Amyntor's concubine (Phthia or Clytia). The fragments of Euripides' version include part of a formal debate (*agōn*) between Amyntor and Phoenix, in which Amyntor was urged to use his knowledge of Phoenix's character, rather than slander or suspicion, as a basis for reasoned judgement (fr. 812). These details seem to correspond quite closely to the plot of *Samia*, but the shortage of evidence makes it impossible to know whether there was a definite intertextual relationship at work. Other tragic intertexts for *Samia* have also been suggested. The myth of Hippolytus, for instance, is structurally very similar to that of Phoenix (a young man is falsely accused of seducing his father's mistress/wife). Euripides wrote two tragedies on the theme – *Hippolytus Veiled* (which is now lost) and *Hippolytus the Garland-Bearer* (the revised version that survives) – and both of these plays have been identified by scholars as possible sources or models for Menander.[34] These are plausible suggestions, but once again the loss of crucial evidence and the absence of any detectable verbal echoes makes them impossible to prove.

As far as we can tell, Demeas never quotes from any of these *Phoenix* or *Hippolytus* tragedies, but he does quote from Euripides' *Oedipus.* It may be thought that any tragic quotation would have done just as well, but I suggest that the choice was not a random one. Note that the quotation is not explicitly acknowledged as such – neither the author nor the play's title is mentioned – and there is nothing about its content that specifically relates to Oedipus. This means (I assume) that not all of the spectators will recognize the reference. But for those who are sufficiently alert and well-read to identify the source, there is another potential layer of humour here. Menander is ever so subtly hinting that the events of *Samia* may echo the myth of Oedipus, who notoriously killed his father (Laius) and unwittingly married his mother (Laius' wife Jocasta). The parallels are not as close as in the cases of Phoenix or Hippolytus, but it is easy to see how Demeas could be loosely assimilated to Laius, Chrysis to Jocasta, and Moschion to Oedipus. Any spectators who do pick up the reference will surely recall it a little later in the play, when Nikeratos directly compares Moschion to Oedipus (496). As far as Nikeratos is concerned, this is a far-fetched comparison made for rhetorical effect,[35] but nonetheless the coincidence is striking. Another striking feature of the plot of *Samia*, which Demeas helpfully reminds us of in lines 346–7, is that Moschion (like Oedipus) is an adopted child. Throughout the play we never learn who his natural parents were, even though this question is bound to occur to us as we play the game of 'what will happen next?' (see pp. 27–30). Another fact that Menander omits to tell us is exactly how old Chrysis is. This is an important – and, I believe, entirely deliberate – omission, since it leaves open the possibility that Chrysis (like Jocasta) is old enough to have a grown-up son. In other words, we are being encouraged to entertain, for a brief moment, the tantalizing possibility that Chrysis will turn out to be Moschion's natural mother. Nothing is made of this possibility in the end, but it would have been a deliciously entertaining plot twist – and the mere hint of it adds piquancy to Demeas' appalled belief that Chrysis has borne Moschion a child.

*

[III.5: *The cook, Demeas, Chrysis*] *The cook emerges, in search of Parmenon, and encounters Demeas on his way indoors. Soon Demeas reappears, and the cook watches as he throws Chrysis, the baby and the old nurse out of the house (357–98).*

The play's defining moment?

Around the same time as the papyrus text of *Samia* was being rediscovered, archaeologists in Mytilene on the island of Lesbos were excavating the so-called 'House of Menander', a private house containing a number of elaborate mosaic floors. The design of one of the mosaics incorporates several separate panels, each featuring an image of Menander or a scene from one of his plays. These mosaics, which were first published in 1970, are hugely valuable for the study of Menander.[36] They not only fill in some details about the characters of several obscure lost works, but they can also – if used with caution – tell us something about the plays' performance style.

Samia is one of eleven comedies depicted (the others are *Encheiridion*, *Epitrepontes*, *Theophoroumenē*, *Kubernētai*, *Leukadia*, *Messenia*, *Misoumenos*, *Plokion*, *Synaristosai*, and *Phasma*). The identification of all these images was unusually easy because the designer of the mosaic had very precisely labelled each scene with the relevant play title as well as the names of the characters. The lettering across the top edge of the *Samia* mosaic reads: CAMIAC ME[POC] Γ MAΓEIPOC ΔHMEAC XPYCIC ('*SAMIA* ACT III – COOK – DEMEAS – CHRYSIS'). The image clearly depicts the masks and costumes of the three characters. The cook wears a black mask with 'dreadlocks', trousers and a brown upper garment. Demeas has a white beard and white hair, and is also dressed in a white robe with long sleeves. Chrysis has golden hair and a headdress, and is wearing a necklace and a bright, multi-coloured robe; she holds the baby in a fold of her upper garment. Because we are now able to look at the image alongside the text itself (something which is impossible in most of the other ten cases), we can be certain that the scene depicted here corresponds precisely to lines 357–98.

Figure 2 The *Samia* mosaic from the House of Menander, Mytilene. From S. Charitōnidēs, L. Kahil and R. Ginouvès, *Les mosaïques de la Maison du Ménandre à Mytilène* (*Antike Kunst-BH* VI, Plate 4.1). Courtesy of the editors of *Antike Kunst*.

Those who have scrutinized this and the other mosaics have concluded that the artist used one of two principles when choosing which scene to illustrate. In each case the scene in question is either the play's opening or its 'defining moment' (i.e. the scene that was thought to have the most visual or thematic impact). Thus the image would have been immediately recognizable by anyone who knew the play, even if their acquaintance with it was only slight. For those who can read, the label offers corroboration and precise context.

In the case of *Samia*, it is easy to see why this particular scene was chosen. The confrontation between Demeas and Chrysis here is structurally central within the plot and seems to mark its emotional climax; Demeas' anger and delusion have reached their extreme limit; Demeas' love for Chrysis has turned to something like hatred, and his callousness towards her is astonishing; Chrysis, distressed, rejected and now homeless, is still clutching the baby to her breast, as in every scene where she appears; and meanwhile the ludicrous comic figure of the cook stands on the periphery, observing their quarrel and making pointless interjections now and then. This distinctive and easily identifiable scene is not just the defining moment of *Samia*, but it could even be seen as a defining illustration of Menander's comic technique. The presence of the cook, a 'stock' figure whose role is simply to generate laughs, during this much more complex and troubling exchange between Demeas and Chrysis causes an odd juxtaposition of contrasting moods. As Stephen Halliwell puts it, 'Menander is demonstrating, as he often likes to, how radically different emotions and viewpoints can coexist side by side within the same social state': it is precisely this technique that generates his characteristic 'fluctuations, intricacies and indeterminacies of tone'.[37] Whoever chose this scene for depiction in art was surely (consciously or unconsciously) recognizing and responding to this key aspect of Menander's work.

The mosaic dates from such a long time after the original performance of *Samia* that it cannot be treated as straightforward evidence for the play's production, either in the fourth century BCE or at the time of the mosaic's manufacture, probably seven or eight hundred years later.[38]

Indeed, it has been thought unlikely that Menander's plays were still being performed on Lesbos, either in theatres or in private settings, as late as the third or fourth century CE.[39] We cannot be sure exactly what these images represent, or why the house-owner decided to decorate his floor with them, or how closely they relate to any specific performances (as opposed to independent products of an artist's imagination, or illustrations from a book). However, the Mytilene mosaics are not unique. In many respects they correspond to other images and theatre-related monuments from all over the Greek world and from a wide variety of dates.[40] It is generally agreed that they are late copies of illustrations that by this time had come to represent a standardized iconography; probably the painters, sculptors, potters and mosaic-makers all used the same archetypes or pattern books. The choice of scenes, the composition of the pictures, the precise details of the masks and costumes – all these elements in the mosaics find close parallels elsewhere in the archaeological record. This means that, even though these particular examples date from many centuries after Menander, the details they depict almost certainly belong to a much earlier period. It has even been suggested that the mosaics are direct descendants of a set of commemorative Athenian wall-paintings from the late fourth century or early third century BCE (that is, contemporary with Menander himself).[41] If this is true, what we see when we look at these three actors in the mosaic – including their costumes, masks and gestures – may be a fairly close approximation to what Menander's original audience would have watched in the theatre in Athens. Of course, it is a long way from being a photographic 'still' of a live performance. It is not even a completely accurate visual record of the scene. (Where is the nurse? Where is the stage building or backdrop? Would the actors really have stood so close together?) But all the same, it gives us a rare and surprisingly vivid glimpse into a vanished world.

*

[III.6: *Chrysis, Nikeratos*] *Demeas retreats indoors and leaves Chrysis in the street. Nikeratos returns from the market, sees her and invites her to stay in his house under the care of his wife until such time as Demeas sees sense. Chrysis, along with the baby and the nurse, follows Nikeratos indoors (399–420).*

Exeunt, pursued by a sheep

As Chrysis stands weeping in the street, Demeas predicts her future with chilling clarity: he expects that she will die of alcoholism or starvation, just like all the other ageing prostitutes who are down on their luck. 'Yes, you'll soon realize who you truly are, and what a mistake you've made!' (390–7). Having delivered these astoundingly vicious exit lines, Demeas makes to go inside, but Chrysis obviously tries to run after him, grab hold of him, or plead with him in some way. Ancient dramatists did not use stage directions, so we cannot tell precisely what Chrysis is doing at this point, but we must infer something of the sort from Demeas' final word: 'Stay where you are!' (*hestathi*, 398). And now, presumably, he slams the door in her face.

In the last few moments before the end of Act III, we see yet another example of Menander's penchant for juxtaposing serious and silly material to create an ambiguous tonal blend. On the one hand, there is a sudden injection of genuine pathos. Chrysis' situation is truly desperate, and it underlines the extreme vulnerability of an unmarried foreign woman without family or male protection. On the other hand, there is also broad humour from a new and unexpected source: a sheep now appears on stage.

The wretched Chrysis cries out, in recognizably tragic style, 'Ah me! How wretched is my fate!' (398). We may be expecting her to launch into a paratragic lament or a monologue about her plight, rather as Demeas did at the start of the last scene, but before she can go any further Nikeratos reappears. He is imagined as having just come back from the market, and he has bought a sheep, which he is dragging behind him. This is bound to raise a laugh. Animals are a perennially popular source of humour, as the Greek comedians well understood.[42]

Just think of all those fifth-century comedies with animal choruses, such as Aristophanes' *Birds*, *Frogs* and *Wasps*, Eupolis' *Goats*, Crates' *Wild Beasts*, Archippus' *Fishes* and so on.[43] No one ever seems to have written a comedy called *Sheep*, though we know of fourth-century comedies with titles such as *The Shepherd* (by Antiphanes) and *The Goatherds* (by Alexis). It is also notable that Cratinus' *Dionysalexandros* featured a shepherd, a character pretending to be a ram and making bleating noises, and other sheep-related silliness.[44] Indeed, Menander himself included a sheep in at least one other play (see *Dyskolos* 393–9).

The introduction of a sheep onto the stage is one of those things that is almost guaranteed to strike the audience as funny. But this is not just any old sheep: Nikeratos goes out of his way to stress the fact that it is a particularly scrawny, undersized, miserable specimen (399–404). He has acquired it especially for the wedding sacrifice, no doubt at a knock-down price, but he complains that once he has finished offering up all the portions conventionally required by the gods – the gall bladder, bones, spleen, blood and so on – there will be nothing left for his guests to eat ... except the fleece! These words show us that the sheep's presence on the scene is not simply gratuitous. It has a ritual function, as a sacrificial victim, and also a practical function, as part of the menu at the wedding banquet. But there was no need for Menander to *show* us the sheep unless he intended to use it for the purpose of entertaining us.

Whenever animals feature in the action (as opposed to the narrative) of ancient drama, we have to think carefully about how this would have been stage-managed. Several tragedies, comedies and satyr-plays seem to call for the use of animals in the theatre, including Aristophanes' *Frogs* and *Wasps* (donkeys), Euripides' *Cyclops* (a herd of sheep and goats), and Euripides' *Hippolytus* and *Helen* (a pack of hunting dogs); many other plays use horse-drawn chariots for the entrances or exits of characters. Were real animals used in each case? Alas, no ancient source can help us answer this question, but the practical difficulties involved are all too easy to imagine. The main problem with using real animals, even if they could be trained to perform after a fashion, is that there would have been no foolproof way of keeping them quiet while they were waiting in the wings or inside the *skēnē* during the other scenes. (Exactly the same problem arises with the use of babies, which is why I assume that Chrysis held a baby doll during all her scenes.) These difficulties would have been all the more acute in the case of tragedy, where an intrusive noise or a momentary lapse into bathos could easily ruin the entire dramatic effect. It is hard to imagine how tragedians solved the problem, but it has been suggested that most of the animals mentioned in the script as if present never physically appeared, and that the spectators were simply required to use their imagination.[45] In comedy, where bathos is allowed (or actively encouraged), and where even a pile of steaming animal dung in the *orchēstra* might not seem out of place, the use of real animals cannot be ruled out. 'Prop' animals on wheels would also be possible. All the same, I suspect that 'extras' dressed as animals could be used if the author wanted a really big laugh. The potential for humour in this scene would be ten times greater if the part of the sheep were taken by an actor wearing a sheep costume, occasionally interjecting bleating noises or being deliberately uncooperative.

But now all the actors, together with the sheep, enter the door of Nikeratos' house, leaving the stage empty for another choral interlude. Once again, as in the case of all these act-dividing songs, the script merely contains the word *CHOROU*, telling us nothing about the music or lyrics (see pp. 41–6), but it is still worth thinking carefully about what style of music would have been most suitable to enhance the theatrical experience at this point. The mood at the end of Act III is a strange mixture of hilarity and desperation, and the plot has now reached its most tangled stage, with the characters all stumbling about in ignorance or afflicted by distress. In Act IV the truth will emerge, and events will start to untangle themselves; but in the meantime we have a pause to sit and reflect as the music plays.

4

Fourth Act

[IV.1: *Nikeratos, Moschion*] *Nikeratos emerges from his house, which he describes as being in a state of turmoil following the arrival of Chrysis and the baby; he criticizes Demeas' behaviour in strong language. Moschion returns, and is appalled when Nikeratos tells him about what has been happening in his absence (421–39).*

A change of pace and a change of rhythm

All of the Greek dialogue in Menander's plays, as in other tragedies and comedies, is composed in verse,[1] and most of it is in iambic trimeter: this metre was considered to be the closest to normal, everyday speech rhythm. The basic pattern of an iambic verse can be illustrated as follows (— stands for a long syllable, ∪ stands for a short syllable, and × marks a syllable that can be either long or short):

× — ∪ — × — ∪ — × — ∪ —

e.g. *Pon-tos pach-eis ger-ont-es ich-thus aph-thon-oi.*[2]

However, different metres might sometimes be used for variety and contrast. The whole of Act IV is composed in catalectic trochaic tetrameter: this metre contains more syllables per line, and has a more energetic feel to it:

— ∪ — × — ∪ — × — ∪ — × — ∪ —

e.g. *ou-chi Chry-sis es-ti mē-tēr hou tre-phei nun pai-di-ou.*[3]

The trochaic meter, which Aristotle thought vulgar and associated with the early origins of drama,[4] tends to mark a distinct change of pace when it is used in either tragedy or comedy. It has even been suggested that dialogue composed in this metre may have been performed in *recitativo* style, set to musical accompaniment (much in the manner of the equivalent metres in Roman comedy).[5] As Gomme and Sandbach observe in their commentary, 'passages in this metre are distinguished in tone from the adjacent iambics, but not always in the same way; they may be marked by excitement, or urgency, or a seriousness that is to be taken seriously.'[6] All of these factors may be thought to apply to Act IV, in which events start to happen thick and fast: this is without doubt the most exciting and lively act of the play.

I begin this chapter by highlighting what may seem to be abstruse technical details because in fact metre is a hugely important element of the play in performance, but it is very easy for readers – especially those with no Greek – to be completely oblivious to it. No English version of *Samia* could hope to reproduce exactly the rhythm and metre of the Greek original. Even if some virtuoso translator could achieve the impressive feat of an English translation with exactly the same number of syllables as the Greek, the essential problem is that the principles of metre are different in each language. English verse is based on the stress or 'beat' (*ictus*), in contrast to Greek verse, which is based on syllabic length. There are several English verse translations of *Samia*, some of which attempt to convey this change of pace by various stylistic means,[7] but in a prose translation, unfortunately, this important aspect is lost altogether – and so, inevitably, the dramatic impact of the scene is diminished.

Obscenity in fourth-century comedy

Nikeratos is so disgusted by Demeas' behaviour towards Chrysis that he resorts to unusually ripe language when describing his old friend. Turning to the audience, he says *Dēmeas skatophagei* (427) – which literally means 'Demeas is eating shit!' As in the case of many other insults in *Samia* (see pp. 75–7), a literal translation does not quite convey the intended meaning, which is obviously something along the lines of 'Demeas is a contemptible fool' (in modern English usage we might simply say: 'Demeas is a shit'). What strikes us especially is Nikeratos' use of a primary obscenity, which is extremely rare in later Greek comedy: only a handful of other comparable expressions can be found.[8] When Menander's characters mention sex at all, they tend to be euphemistic rather than explicit – as, for instance, when Moschion makes his stumbling confession in Act I (47–50: see pp. 21–3). This marks a complete contrast with Aristophanes and fifth-century comedy, in which sexual and excremental language is so pervasive as to be seen as a defining feature of the genre.[9] Whenever we encounter an obscenity in Aristophanes we may or may not be offended, but we will not really be surprised. It is precisely because Menander's language is normally so decorous and restrained that this rare lapse is utterly shocking. We can see at once that Nikeratos must be extraordinarily angry. The placing of the surprising word at the very beginning of the act makes it stand out even more: this is another way, apart from the metre, in which Menander signals to the audience that Act IV marks a change of pace.

As Jeffrey Henderson puts it (in *The Maculate Muse*, the standard reference work on the subject), 'obscenity in Attic comedy seems to have been an indispensable feature of the genre. Its importance as a potent vehicle for ridicule, abuse, satire and comic exposure could not be equaled by any other weapon in the poet's arsenal.'[10] Henderson makes a persuasive case for regarding obscenity as inherently linked to political comedy. If we see obscene language as a facet of democratic free speech, it is easy to understand its decline as a direct result of the erosion of democracy and the political instability that characterized fourth-century Athens. Apparently there was no censorship as such: the fact that Menander could still insert a rude word here and there, if he wanted to do so, shows that there was no prohibition on the use of bad language in fourth-century comedy (in contrast to most forms of entertainment media throughout the twentieth century in British and American society). But, in Henderson's view, 'without its function in the humor of abuse and exposure, obscenity becomes mere smut and disappears'. Obviously smut or toilet humour for its own sake didn't appeal very strongly to Menander or his audience.

The long day of comedy

Moschion now reappears after his period of solitary reflection, and he is talking to himself as he enters the stage (428–30).

> Is the sun *never* going to set? What's going on? Has night forgotten itself? Oh, how long the afternoon seems! I shall go and take a bath – for the third time – because I can't think of anything else to do.

He is self-consciously drawing attention to a convention of Greek drama – the so-called 'unity of time' – which dictated that the entire action of a play should normally take place during a single day.[11] The convention (together with the 'unity of place') represents the norm in fifth-century tragedy, and may be accounted for by the fact that tragic choruses almost always remain on stage for the whole duration of the performance. Aristophanes sometimes breaks the rule, but Menander always observes it. This is one among several ways in which, as we have already seen, Menander's comedy shows close affinities to tragedy. Nick Lowe, in a useful survey of the evolution of Greek comedy, sees 'the abandonment of Old Comedy's freer stage conventions for the austere literalism of tragedy' as one of the most important differences between fourth- and fifth-century comedy.[12] But scenes like this one show that Menander's adoption of the convention need not always be austere.[13] By making Moschion deliberately allude to the convention and emphasize its artificiality, Menander is transforming it into a metatheatrical joke.

Moschion is drawing our attention specifically to the fact that in *Samia*, as in so many other comedies, a lot of plot has to be squeezed into the play's single day. Relationships change and develop with unnatural rapidity; the characters' fortunes see-saw up and down constantly; plot twists and revelations proliferate. If every day were like this, life would be unbearably exhausting. Even though comedy adheres to the one-day rule, its handling of dramatic time is inevitably somewhat ambiguous and elastic in order to accommodate everything that has to happen. Usually we are not supposed to enquire too deeply into exactly how much time has passed during an act or scene. If we start thinking about it, we soon realize that the notional duration of a scene, or of a character's temporary absence from the stage, or of a choral interlude, cannot correspond to real time. For instance, during Act IV Nikeratos repeatedly goes in and out of his house – at lines 520, 532, 547, 556, 563, 570 and 614 – while continuous action and dialogue are taking place on the stage: is Nikeratos really given enough time in between his appearances to do what he is supposedly doing inside the house? (Surely not.) Sometimes time can seem to slow down as well as speed up. Moschion left the stage not so very long ago, in the middle of Act II (161–2), yet he seems to have had enough time to go to the public baths not once but twice. He must be *extremely* clean by now, though he has a further bath to look forward to – his ritual marriage bath, which will follow at the end of Act V (729).

The idea that the sun has somehow forgotten to set, or that day or night might be freakishly extended to accommodate a busy comic plot, is a nice conceit. Like many nice ideas in Menander, it is recycled from earlier drama. The same motif was used by Plautus in his *Amphitryo*, our sole surviving example of 'mythological' comedy from antiquity. In that play it is not simply mentioned as a theoretical (im)possibility but used as a central plot device: the god Jupiter really does suspend the clock in order to give himself an extra-long night of passion with Amphitryo's wife Alcumena. *Amphitryo* is a Roman comedy, dating from the early second century BCE, but it was based on Greek models – including (probably) Platon's comedy *The Long Night*.[14]

*

[IV.2: *Nikeratos, Moschion, Demeas*] *Demeas is still determined that the marriage of Moschion and Plangon shall take place. He turns to the altar of Apollo and prays that the god may help him to celebrate the wedding cheerfully and hide his anger. Moschion approaches his father, demands to know why he has ejected Chrysis, and urges him to take her back. Demeas reveals that he knows that Moschion is the baby's father, and Moschion admits it, not realizing that Demeas also believes Chrysis to be the baby's mother. Nikeratos and Demeas now both believe that Moschion has had an affair with Chrysis, and they condemn his behaviour in exaggeratedly strong terms. Nikeratos regards Chrysis as disgracefully immoral, and decides that she must leave his house forthwith, so he goes inside to fetch her. Taking advantage of Nikeratos' temporary absence, Moschion finally confesses to his father that the baby's parents are himself and Plangon (440–532).*

Attitudes to sexual morality

In this long scene the three principal male characters come face to face for the first time. Because they are all labouring under misapprehensions to a greater or lesser degree, they end up bandying words at cross purposes, becoming more and more angry with one another as the scene progresses. Because we spectators know the full truth about the situation, we can enjoy the dramatic irony that arises from watching the characters' misunderstandings. But it is also worth paying attention to exactly what the characters say whenever the subject of sex or marriage comes up. Even though they completely misunderstand the specifics of the situation, their words and reactions reveal their underlying attitudes to gender and sexual morality in a more general sense. Presumably what they say represents the sort of opinion that ordinary Athenian men of Menander's time might hold.[15]

All three men agree on the principle that for a man to sleep with another man's wife or *pallakē*, or for a wife or *pallakē* to sleep with another man, is a very wicked thing indeed. They all repeatedly use the same adjective when talking about it – *deinos* ('terrible', 454, 456, 462, 490) or the strengthened form *pandeinos* ('utterly terrible', 487, 495). This is not simply a question of private morality: it reflects the fact that in Athenian law adultery was one of the most serious crimes, which could be judged worthy of capital punishment.[16] It was up to the cuckolded husband, as the perceived victim in the case, to exact the appropriate penalty. Even though Demeas is not married to Chrysis, he behaves exactly as if he were her husband, and he describes both Chrysis and Moschion as having committed a crime (*adikia*) against him (329, 456, 518). Several scholars have noted the similarities between Demeas' presentation of the 'facts in the case' and real-life legal speeches on the same subject, such as Lysias 1 (*On the Killing of Eratosthenes*).[17] Note that throughout this scene Demeas keeps turning for support to the men in the audience (447, 461, 488). As we have already observed in relation to earlier scenes, this sort of rhetoric almost seems to give the impression that we are in a law court. But Demeas also turns more than once to the god Apollo (444, 474–5), whose altar and effigy stand by the door of his house. These repeated gestures are not there simply to create a legalistic flavour: they show us that Demeas confidently expects confirmation from his fellow Athenian citizens and from the gods that his attitude is completely reasonable and normal.

Whether Moschion or Chrysis bears the greater share of responsibility is naturally an ambiguous question (see 456, 473–5, 479–80, 482, and compare Demeas' earlier agonized words at 327–49). Nevertheless, Moschion, the apple of his adoptive father's eye, is given the benefit of the doubt, and Chrysis is the one who ends up paying the penalty. The belief that an unfaithful woman should be rejected by her man and removed from the household is accepted without question. Nikeratos' initial criticism of Demeas' treatment of Chrysis (426–7) arises purely from the fact that it seems inexplicable at the time. When, later in the scene, he discovers Demeas' reason for rejecting Chrysis, he no longer criticizes him but behaves in precisely the same way towards her. Demeas actively encourages him in this course, saying: 'Throw her out, Nikeratos, I beseech you! Take your proper share in this injustice, like a true friend' (518). In other words, it is assumed that Nikeratos, as a friend (*philos*) of the victim, automatically becomes a victim himself, with a duty to join in avenging the 'crime'.

Nikeratos' reaction is comically exaggerated, in order to provide an amusing contrast with Demeas, but he essentially reflects exactly the same sort of outlook. Launching into paratragic style, he denounces Moschion as the equivalent of the worst villains of Greek mythology: 'Oh! The sexual crimes of Tereus, Oedipus, Thyestes and all the rest of them – yes, all the atrocities that we have ever heard about – you have made them all seem insignificant by comparison!' (495–6). Warming to his theme, Nikeratos marvels that Moschion could have dared to commit such a crime, and he urges Demeas to do what the tragic king Amyntor did and blind his son as a punishment (498–500). Furthermore, he declares that he himself would have meted out a much more severe punishment to anyone who had dishonoured his bed: 'On the very next day, quicker than anyone else, I would have sold the mistress into slavery – and I would have auctioned off my son at the same time!' (508–10). The selling of free men and women into slavery was itself a capital offence,[18] so what Nikeratos is proposing is blatantly illegal; but he claims that no one in Athens would blame him in the slightest, because what Moschion has done is *murder* (513–14):

> **Demeas** Murder? What do you mean, 'murder'?
>
> **Nikeratos** It's murder, in my judgement, when someone rises up and does something like this!

Even Demeas obviously thinks that Nikeratos is going wildly over the top, as indeed he is. Perhaps Nikeratos himself realizes this, because it is at this point that he turns the blame on Chrysis, describing her as 'the perpetrator of these terrible crimes' (516) and vowing to throw her out on the streets again.

Where the two old men really differ from one another is in their attitude to Nikeratos' daughter Plangon. Demeas, even though he believes his son to be guilty of a sexual misdemeanour, is (astonishingly) still happy for him to marry Plangon, and he wants to get on with the wedding ceremony as soon as possible (469–71). But Nikeratos has no intention of allowing his daughter to marry such a man: 'Is there anybody whose bed you would not defile? Am I really going to give my own daughter to you?' (501–2). As Moschion stands there listening to Nikeratos, he says, in an 'aside' to the audience, that he is frozen with fear – as well he might be (515). How will Nikeratos react when he finds out that Moschion has had sex with Plangon and given her a child?

Since almost all the attention is fixed on Moschion's imaginary crime, it is easy to forget about his actual sexual misconduct, even though this is likely to strike us as a much more serious matter.[19] But when the subject of Moschion's rape or seduction of Plangon does indirectly enter the conversation, it is made clear that this is regarded – by Moschion himself, at least – as a much less serious offence (525–6). When Moschion thinks that Demeas is confronting him with the knowledge of what he has done to Plangon, he freely admits to it, and offers an excuse (486–7):

> But it isn't an utterly terrible thing, father:
> after all, countless men have done the same thing.

In contrast to his earlier speech, in which he did show genuine embarrassment (if not remorse) for his behaviour, Moschion now adopts the line that his behaviour was completely unexceptionable; he seems to imply that no normal person could possibly criticize him. Perhaps we are to imagine that his behaviour is excused or mitigated by the fact that he intends to marry Plangon and make everything respectable, though he doesn't exactly say so.[20]

If Moschion did rape Plangon, these lines will seem completely outrageous – to most modern readers, at least. As we have already observed (pp. 24–7), ancient and modern ways of understanding sex and sexual consent are so different that we cannot trust our own reactions as a guide to what Menander's spectators might have thought. Nevertheless, I suspect that Moschion's words will have been a little difficult to swallow even for an audience of fourth-century Athenian men. Did 'countless men' really go about raping women? Did they all marry their victims after they had given birth to children? Are we really meant to view sexual relationships like this one as common or even normative? It seems very unlikely that we can treat what Moschion says as an accurate reflection of the social world of contemporary Athens. Perhaps it is better to treat it as a self-conscious metatheatrical comment on comic formulas and plot conventions.

It is important to acknowledge that all these relationships are seen through male eyes. We are dealing exclusively with men describing or evaluating sexual conduct in front of other men.[21] Tellingly, Menander never shows us an equivalent scene in which three female characters discuss the same sort of questions. At the same time as this long scene is unfolding before us, we can imagine that the women inside Nikeratos' house – who now include Chrysis and the old nurse as well as Nikeratos' wife and daughter – are also talking about the situation among themselves. Indeed, Nikeratos indirectly acknowledges that this is so when he says: 'There are tears being shed; the women have been making a racket' (426), though his contemptuous language shows his total lack of interest in what they were actually saying. Nevertheless, some of us will perhaps be wondering whether the women's perspective on sexual relationships differs from the men's. It is certainly striking that the women are depicted as more compassionate and more willing to forgive perceived sexual misconduct. As soon as the men suspect Chrysis of unfaithfulness, they immediately respond by ejecting her from the household, thus effectively nullifying her as a person; but by contrast, the women in Nikeratos' household accept her and show her kindness. Similarly, Chrysis is ready to overlook irregularities in the sexual relationship of Moschion and Plangon; she is simply sympathetic and supportive, and actively helps them try to put matters right. It is hard to avoid concluding that the women come out of this affair in a far more favourable light than the male characters.

Who is Diomnestus?

The standard textbooks and scholarly accounts of the development of Greek comedy all highlight two key features of the genre that more or less disappeared after the end of the fifth century: obscenity and personal mockery. Artistic styles and popular tastes naturally evolve over time, and it is hard to pinpoint the exact causes behind these disappearances, but political uncertainty and regime changes in Athens throughout the fourth century are commonly invoked as explanations. *Samia* is of interest to historians of the theatre because it contains vestiges of both these obsolescent features. In Act IV we have already been surprised by a burst of obscenity from Nikeratos (see pp. 90–2), and now we encounter the first of three disparaging references to real-life Athenian individuals. When Nikeratos, in a rage, vows that no daughter of his will ever marry Moschion, he declares that he would rather take Diomnestus as a son-in-law (504).

It would help us to understand the exact point of the joke if we knew who Diomnestus was. The name Diomnestus is attested elsewhere in classical Athens, but little is known about any specific holders of that name.[22] Obviously this particular Diomnestus must have been sufficiently well known for the mere mention of his name to convey the desired meaning. The joke would be more amusing if Diomnestus was a famously bad husband or a self-evidently unsuitable candidate for a son-in-law. Was he a notorious bigamist? Had he recently been convicted of murdering his wife or his father-in-law? Had he appeared in a high-profile adultery case? Had he been disgraced for having sex with other men? We can do little more than speculate (as a glance at any of the commentaries will confirm). However, we need not even assume that Diomnestus had a specific connection with marriage: perhaps he was simply a well-known or controversial public figure. The structure of the joke – 'Moschion is bad, but X is worse' – is such that almost any famous name (X) could be inserted into it and still get a laugh. So the identity of Diomnestus remains a mystery.

An equally important but equally mysterious question is why Menander was so eager to make fun of Diomnestus here that he temporarily abandoned his normal habit of excluding all references to the real world outside the play. Exactly why does he do it here but almost nowhere else? Was the reference so apposite that he couldn't resist the temptation? It's difficult to believe that this fleeting, half-hearted allusion was worth the effort. It lacks satirical point, it isn't developed in any detail, and it isn't particularly funny: it barely even counts as mockery at all.

Much the same can be said of the other two personal references in Act IV. At line 603 Demeas refers in passing to 'Chaerephon, who eats at other people's expense'. In this case the target of the mockery can be more easily identified – Chaerephon, who is made fun of elsewhere in comedy, was a famous glutton, who is often compared to the comic figure of the parasite – but the reference seems perfunctory as well as largely irrelevant to the context.[23] A few lines later (606–9) Demeas mentions one Androcles, who is described as being youthful and dark-haired in spite of his great age. There have been various inconclusive attempts to identify this person with known historical figures, but once again the point of the reference is obscure.[24]

All these personal references are limited to the briefest of passing moments. They draw attention to themselves because of their scarcity, but it cannot be claimed that they are central to the meaning or the humour of the scene. In fact, they seem rather pointless and puzzling. But it is striking to find them at all in a late fourth-century comedy. It is hard to explain exactly why Menander decided to insert these jokes, but the fact that he did tells us one important fact: it shows that the comedians' freedom of speech had not been completely curtailed at the time of writing. Additionally, the reference to Chaerephon has been seen as a rough indication of the play's date, in the absence of any external evidence, since all the other comic references to this individual seem to cluster around the years *c.* 325 to *c.* 310.[25]

*

[IV.3: *Nikeratos, Demeas, Moschion*] *Nikeratos rushes out of the house, aghast after discovering Plangon breast-feeding the baby: he is appalled by the realization that his daughter has borne an illegitimate child. Moschion, panicking, flees the scene (533–67).*

The importance of stage directions

This scene is unusually complicated in terms of stagecraft. The configuration of the action, the interrelation of the three characters, and the delivery of the dialogue require careful attention. What makes the scene difficult – though far from atypical – is that it relies on dramatic convention rather than strict realism.[26] The characters do not behave naturally or consistently. To the audience they might look like three normal people sharing the same confined space, but for the purposes of the scene they show only selective and intermittent awareness of one another. At the same time they intermittently either acknowledge or ignore the spectators. To a theatre audience familiar with the conventions of comic stagecraft, none of this would seem very difficult or unusual, but readers have to work much harder to process what is going on.

[*532–3*] Nikeratos emerges from the doorway. He temporarily assumes a 'tragic' role, uttering a lament in paratragic language. He seems to be addressing his words to the audience at this point; if he is aware of Demeas or Moschion, he does not acknowledge their presence. It is not clear how far apart the characters are, but I take it that Demeas and Moschion are somewhere towards the edge of the stage (if not in the *orchēstra* itself), sufficiently distant from Nikeratos and the *skēne* to make this 'selective deafness' more plausible.[27]

[*535a*][28] Demeas interrupts Nikeratos' lament with the question: 'Whatever will he say next?' It is unclear whether this utterance represents an 'aside' to himself or the audience, notionally inaudible to the other characters, or a direct question to Moschion, notionally inaudible to Nikeratos. Dramatic convention dictates that Demeas cannot speak at exactly the same time as Nikeratos. The formal metrical structure of the verses must continue unbroken, which means that Demeas is given the first four syllables of 535 before Nikeratos continues speaking the remainder of the verse.

[*535b–536a*] Nikeratos gives no sign that he has heard Demeas' interjection. He continues with his narrative of events in the house, and (presumably) still addresses the audience, but he now drops the tragic language and returns to a more usual informal style of speech.[29] Throughout all this Moschion and Demeas are obviously able to see and hear everything that Nikeratos does and says.

[*536b*] Either Moschion or Demeas interrupts, saying: 'So that's what he meant!' As at 535a, this might be an 'aside' or a comment directly addressed to another character, but it is obviously meant to be inaudible to Nikeratos. The reason why the speaker's identity is uncertain is that the papyrus text would normally use a mark called the dicolon (:) to indicate each change of speaker, but no such mark appears at the end of 536. Thus we would normally assume that Moschion is the speaker, and that 536b and 537a together form a single utterance. However, someone or other has added the abbreviation *Mosch.* in the margin of the papyrus at line 537, and most recent editors (following Jean-Marie Jacques in his 1971 Budé text) attribute 536b to Demeas and 537a to Moschion. (See below for further discussion and illustration of the text at this crucial point.)

[*537a*] The first part of this line – 'Do you hear that, father?' – is unquestionably spoken by Moschion. But if Demeas *is* the speaker of 536b, Moschion's words do not seem like a reply to the words 'So that's what he meant!' So we must assume that Moschion either failed to hear Demeas' words or chooses to ignore them, or that 536b is addressed to the audience (and is inaudible to both Nikeratos and Moschion).

[*537b–538a*] Demeas turns to Moschion and directly addresses him: 'Moschion, you are innocent of wrongdoing, but I have wronged you by suspecting you of such things.' This moment of recognition marks a major turning point in the plot, and it clears the way for the damaged relationship between father and son to be mended. It would be natural for Demeas' words to be accompanied by an emotionally expressive gesture such as an embrace or an outstretched hand, though the text gives no direct sign of this.

[*538b*] At this point Nikeratos suddenly becomes aware of Demeas' presence, but he is apparently still oblivious to the presence of Moschion, who is right beside him. Nikeratos addresses only Demeas, supplying

his own 'stage direction' in his words: 'Demeas, I come to you!' He leaves the doorway of his house and approaches Demeas at the edge of the stage.

[*539a*] Moschion, in an 'aside', unheard by Nikeratos, exclaims, 'I'm out of here!' Presumably he starts to move off stage by one of the gangways, notionally in the direction of the city. Nikeratos makes no sign that he can see or hear Moschion.

[*539b*] Demeas interjects a single word, *tharrei* – 'Courage!' – which must be addressed to Moschion but inaudible to Nikeratos.

[*539c*] Moschion adds the words: 'I'm as good as dead when I look at him!' Since he has no more lines, we must take it that he exits at this point. We also note the extremely rapid speaker-changes in this verse, which is divided into three separate utterances while maintaining the strict verse rhythm.

[*540a*] Demeas directly asks Nikeratos: 'What's the matter?'

[*540b–541*] Nikeratos tells Demeas exactly the same information that he has just narrated at 535–6: he clearly does not realize that Demeas has heard him doing so.

[*542–544a*] A normal exchange of dialogue between Nikeratos and Demeas, in which each hears and directly responds to the other's words.

[*544b–545a*] Demeas, coming to terms fully with his knowledge of the situation, says: 'I am responsible for all this!' His words must be audible to the audience, but they are not completely audible to Nikeratos.

[*545b*] Nikeratos asks Demeas: 'What are you saying?' showing that he has heard something but not Demeas' exact words.

[*545c–546a*] Demeas pretends to repeat what he said, but in fact he says something different: 'What you're telling me seems unbelievable!' Nikeratos protests that he really did see Plangon feeding the baby, but Demeas refuses to accept it.

[*546b–547a*] Nikeratos begins a sentence in reply to Demeas, but breaks off halfway through: 'This is not make-believe! I'll go back inside and . . .' This utterance is clearly incomplete, but Demeas starts talking again anyway.

[*547b*] Demeas says: 'I tell you what . . .' (*to deina*). This is what linguisticians refer to as a pragmatic marker (defined as 'constructions that are present in speech to support interaction but do not generally add any specific semantic meaning to the sentence').[30] Such utterances can be used, as here, to signal a change of subject and grab the listener's attention. In other words, Demeas is being selectively deaf again, or the interrupted sentence was delivered as an aside. Either he is ignoring Nikeratos' last words or he failed to hear them altogether: he just wants to talk about something different. Demeas does not notice at once that Nikeratos has left the stage in the middle of their conversation, but by the time he does so it is too late. 'Just a minute, my dear chap . . . oh, he's gone.'

I have spent some time (perhaps too much time, some will think) spelling out exactly what is happening on stage at each moment here. This is to demonstrate the importance of stage directions for anyone who approaches this scene via the medium of the printed page. Menander's script contains only the characters' words, but by themselves these words are not always enough: we need to envisage the scene in performance in order for it to make total sense. It hardly needs saying that this sort of micro-description of the action and dialogue would be wearisome to read at length, and it would fill considerably more pages than the text of the play itself. It is easy to see why published translations, which are primarily aimed at readers and students rather than actors and directors, use only minimal (and therefore inadequate) stage directions. It is also easy for readers to forget that any stage directions in a published edition are the work of the editor or translator, not Menander himself. Sometimes there may be room for debate or disagreement. It is up to each of us to read attentively and use our own imagination.

Book-readers in antiquity faced even greater challenges.[31] Ancient books and manuscripts of dramatic works used virtually no stage directions.[32] Even such basic information as the name of the speaker is omitted in many cases: readers were expected to work it out for themselves. If we are lucky we will find that a change of speaker is indicated by a *paragraphos* (a horizontal line) in between verses, or a *dicolon* (:) if the speaker changes in the middle of a verse, but these marks are not always consistently used. Nor did ancient texts typically provide what we nowadays think of as indispensable aids to the reader, such as punctuation marks, spaces in between the words, or a mixture of upper- and lower-case letters. To illustrate how difficult and off-putting this style of presentation can be, here are lines 535–7 exactly as they appear in Bodmer Papyrus XXV:[33]

> ΤΙΠΟΤ’ΕΡΕΙ:ΤΗΝΘΥΓΑΤΕΡΑΤΗΝΕΜΗΝΤΩΠΑΙΔΙΩΙ
ΤΙΤΘΙΟΝΔΙΔΟΥΣΑΝΕΝΔΟΝΚΑΤΕΛΑΒΟΝ:ΤΟΥΤ’ΗΝΑΡΑ·
ΠΑΤΕΡΑΚΟΥΕΙΣ:ΟΥΔΕΝΑΔΙΚΕΙΣΜΟΣΧΙΩΝ·ΕΓΩΔΕΣΕ

The equivalent in English would look something like this:

> WHATEVERWILLHESAYNEXT:JUSTNOWICAUGHTMYDAUGHTER
INSIDESUCKLINGTHEBABY:SOTHATSWHATHEMEANT
DOYOUHEARTHATFATHER:MOSCHIONYOUAREINNOCENTBUTI

It will be clear that we twenty-first-century scholars and students are considerably better off than our ancient counterparts, but we still need to be constantly aware that reading *Samia* (or any ancient drama) is a very different sort of experience from watching it in performance.

Noisy doors

There is one stage direction in particular that does not need to be reconstructed by inference, because it is explicitly included in the characters' words. This is the curiously loud noise that the doors sometimes make when they are about to open.

Scholars have debated inconclusively whether the noise is caused by creaky hinges, inward or outward opening, rattling bolts or the impact of the door banging against its frame; but perhaps they are missing the point if they are looking for strict verisimilitude.[34] The point is that these scripted noises are ludicrously *un*realistic. The way in which the characters repeatedly draw attention to the door noise is a well-established comic routine, seen frequently in many other Greek and Roman dramas.[35] It is a useful way of announcing a character's sudden entrance, but more importantly it is a silly device for generating humour. It may well be that each mention of the noise was accompanied by some sort of sound effect to exaggerate the silliness.

Samia makes more use of this old chestnut than any other extant comedy. We first encounter the motif at line 300, but it is repeated five more times after that (at 366, 532, 555, 567 and 669). We may or may not consciously notice that the front doors of both houses are equally noisy, but we will be aware that the doors do not creak or rattle every time someone opens them: this confirms that it is a deliberate, self-conscious motif, to be deployed only when the comic timing is suitable.[36] Each subsequent occurrence increases our awareness that the motif is being used as a running gag, and makes it seem more and more ridiculous. In Act IV the door makes its noise more frequently than elsewhere, with three occurrences clustering together in this short scene. This may seem appropriate for what is an especially exciting, fast-paced section of the play, but it also increases the sense of artificiality and self-consciousness. At the end of the scene, just before Chrysis comes running out of Nikeratos' house, Demeas breaks off what he is saying and exclaims: 'By Apollo! The door is creaking *again*!' (567).

*

[IV.4: *Chrysis, Demeas, Nikeratos*] *Chrysis, holding the baby close for protection, runs out of Nikeratos' house, with Nikeratos in pursuit, brandishing a stick. Before Nikeratos can seize the baby, Demeas tells Chrysis to go back inside his own house. Nikeratos threatens Demeas with violence, and the two old friends come to blows (568–75).*

A reconciliation?

This scene passes so quickly that we might almost fail to notice a major plot development taking place. The main focus is on the physical confrontation between the two old men, which degenerates into a fistfight (574–81). But at the same time what we seem to be witnessing here is a reconciliation – of sorts – between Demeas and Chrysis. Bearing in mind Demeas' appalling treatment of Chrysis in Act III, and the fact that he was entirely to blame for making a mistake, we may be expecting that some form of protracted emotional reunion will follow. Will Demeas issue a grovelling apology? Will he shower Chrysis with sweet talk and promises of gifts? Far from it. Instead, what we hear is this (569):

Demeas Over here, Chrysis!

Chrysis Who's calling me?

Demeas Get inside, quickly!

We don't realize it yet, but this is Chrysis' final speaking appearance on stage. She goes back inside Demeas' house and does not emerge again (unless she appears as a mute character in the final scene): thus we must take it that she will ultimately be reinstated in her former position as *pallakē* and mistress of the household.[37] But why does Menander make so little of this key moment?

It is tempting to see it as a missed opportunity. Perhaps Menander was simply running out of steam by this point in the plot, or perhaps he had lost interest in Chrysis and her situation: after all, even though she gives the play its title, she was never really the main character. Alternatively, we could see this surprising shift of focus away from Chrysis as entirely deliberate. Perhaps it is another example of 'the comedy of disappointment', whereby Menander purposely raises and then frustrates his audience's expectations.[38] Either way, the lack of a satisfying conclusion to Chrysis' story is a conspicuous loose end that Menander leaves dangling at the end of the play. It is hard not to feel that kind, admirable, self-sacrificing Chrysis, after all that she has so unfairly suffered, has been cheated of a happy ending.[39] Is it too anachronistic to imagine that this is Menander's way of making us feel sympathy for Chrysis and other women like her?[40]

*

[IV.5: *Nikeratos, Demeas*] *Demeas prevents Nikeratos from going inside and tries to calm him down. Now that Nikeratos knows the full truth about the baby's parentage, Demeas uses a parallel from tragedy to persuade him that life is full of unexpected happenings and that Moschion will be a suitable husband for Plangon. Nikeratos finally returns to his house intending to resume the preparations for the wedding, and Demeas thanks the gods that all his suspicions proved to be unfounded (576–615).*

Lessons from tragedy

In the course of Act IV the truth finally emerges and the characters' misapprehensions are put right, but it still remains for them to come to terms with everything that has happened. 'Come and take a little walk with me,' says Demeas to his old friend (587–8). As the two men stroll up and down, Demeas tries to help Nikeratos calm down and accept the situation for what it is. His chosen method of doing so is to quote an illustration from tragedy (588–98):

Demeas Pull yourself together now. Tell me, Nikeratos, have you not heard the tragedians tell how Zeus transformed himself into gold, poured through the roof and had his wicked way with a young girl locked up in a chamber?

Nikeratos Yes, but what of it?

Demeas That shows us, perhaps, that we need to be prepared for any eventuality. Think about it: is your roof leaking at all?

Nikeratos Yes, most of it leaks. But how are these two things connected?

Demeas Zeus sometimes comes as gold, sometimes as water. Do you see? What's happened is down to him. How easily we've worked it out!

Nikeratos Oh, you're making an idiot of me.

Demeas No, by Apollo, I'm not! What I mean is this. Surely you're in no way inferior to Acrisius. And if he deemed *his* daughter worthy of honour, then . . .

In other words, the underlying general principle is that tragedy can be beneficial in one of two ways: it can be a source of comfort and consolation in times of distress, and it can help one understand one's own situation better by furnishing analogies or parallels from the world of myth.

The specific mythic paradigm being cited is that of the Argive princess Danae. This was a very popular subject among fifth-century dramatists, and Demeas' vague reference to 'the tragedians' might encompass any or all of Aeschylus' *Polydectes* (or his satyr-play *Net-Fishers*), Sophocles' *Acrisius*, *Danae* or *Men of Larissa*, or Euripides' *Danae* or *Dictys*.[41] All these plays are now lost, though a few fragments survive, and the myth is well known from other literary sources. Danae's father Acrisius, having received an oracle telling him that any son born to Danae would kill him, shut his daughter up in an underground chamber. Zeus fell in love with Danae, entered the chamber in the form of a golden shower and impregnated her, and she later gave birth to a son (Perseus). According to Demeas, this constitutes an excellent parallel to the situation in hand. If Nikeratos comes to realize that his situation is just like that of Acrisius, then surely he will forgive Moschion and rejoice in the unexpected good fortune of having a 'divine' grandson. Furthermore, the inconvenient fact that Plangon has been seduced or raped is perhaps desensitized, or made to seem more palatable, by its assimilation to a remote mythical fantasy.[42]

If only the parallel were so close. In fact, if we happen to have even a basic familiarity with any of these tragedies, it will immediately occur to us that Demeas' choice of the Danae myth is rhetorically inept. Acrisius, when he discovered that he had been landed with a grandson despite his precautions, did not happily acquiesce in the situation, as Nikeratos is being expected to do. He locked Danae and the infant Perseus in a chest and threw them into the sea! Nikeratos appears to be unaware of this fact, and perhaps it is implied that Demeas himself is equally ignorant. But since the Danae myth was such a well-known one, we can assume that many of Menander's spectators would have realized that this is actually an ironical joke at the expense of one or both of the characters.

All the same, the underlying principle – that tragedy can (in theory) have beneficial or therapeutic effects on its spectators or readers – is not being questioned. This is a genuinely important concept in Greek literary criticism, and close connections can be seen between Menander and other contemporary writers who discuss the topic – including Plato and Aristotle as well as other fourth-century comedians.[43] In several respects Demeas' and Nikeratos' conversation about the relationship between tragedy and real life is strikingly similar to a surviving passage from Timocles' lost comedy *Women Celebrating the Dionysia* (fr. 6 K–A):

> Listen, my dear fellow, and find out if I have something worth saying. Man is a creature naturally prone to suffering, and life is full of woes. This is why man invented these distractions from cares. For, when the mind forgets about its own concerns and is distracted by somebody else's suffering, it goes away feeling pleasure and is also educated at the same time. First of all, if you will, just consider how the tragedians benefit everyone. A poor man, when he learns that Telephus was even more of a beggar than himself, bears his poverty more easily. The man who is afflicted by madness can consider Alcmeon. If someone has eye-disease – the sons of Phineus are blind. If someone's child has died – Niobe has lightened his load. If someone is lame – he can look at Philoctetes. An old man down on his luck can learn a lesson from Oeneus. When anyone considers that all these misfortunes, greater than his own, have happened to others, he groans less about his own problems.

Timocles' version of this theme, which scholars have interpreted specifically in the light of Aristotle's theory of *katharsis*, is not precisely the same as Menander's version, which is less explicit as well as more obviously ironical. But essentially both poets seem to be drawing on the same sort of ideas about the practical lessons and psychological benefits to be derived from tragedy.

This strand in *Samia* marks another way, quite distinct from what we have already discussed, in which Menander deploys tragedy for comic purposes. As before, the characters continue to behave as if 'life is like a tragedy'.[44] But now they are seen as not simply living through tragic-style events as participants. They are also commentators, able to stand outside the tragic scenario and talk about it with a degree of critical detachment. Furthermore, they are assumed to be *au fait* with contemporary intellectual debates about the nature and purpose of tragedy. But it is hard to decide how seriously Menander is engaging with the sphere of literary criticism, just as it is hard to decide whether Menander's comedies are seriously philosophical.[45] Is there a 'point' to be made, or is Menander just having fun?

5

Fifth Act

Since all fourth-century comedies conventionally had five acts, by this point the audience can be certain that the end is in sight.[1] Most of the mess and misunderstanding has already been cleared up, which means that during the choral interlude we will have been reflecting on what Menander will do next in order to bring the play to a satisfying conclusion. If we are familiar with any of Menander's other comedies (especially *Dyskolos* and *Epitrepontes*), we may also be reflecting that he likes to use the fifth act to tease his audiences, postponing the *dénouement* by adding further complications to a situation that already seemed to have been resolved. We can be fairly confident that the long-postponed wedding of Moschion and Plangon will – eventually – be allowed to take place, but what else might happen in the meantime? As we have already noted, there remain several tantalizing loose ends with the potential for development – including the question of whether we will be treated to a revelation about Chrysis' or Moschion's real identity. We will also recall that Moschion, who fled the scene during the previous act, is still under the impression that Nikeratos is going to prevent him from marrying Plangon: he doesn't realize that the wedding preparations are again under way.

Comic closure

The desire of theatre audiences and readers for narrative closure is a phenomenon that has been widely discussed. Classic treatments of the subject include Roland Barthes' *The Pleasure of the Text*, Frank Kermode's *The Sense of an Ending*, June Schlueter's *Dramatic Closure:*

Reading the End and D.A. Miller's *Narrative and its Discontents*.[2] None of these works deals specifically with classical literature or drama, but the sort of questions and issues that they raise are pertinent to Menander.[3] How do literary works end? Does the genre of a work determine the sort of ending that it has? Why might certain endings be described as 'open' or 'closed'? What counts as a 'happy' ending, and is it the same as a fully resolved one? In what sense is the end of a literary work final, given that the characters' lives are imagined as continuing after the last page or scene? What are the implications of endings for us, the readers, as well as the characters? Is closure synonymous with conclusion? How does closure affect the meaning of a work in interpretative terms? These are crucial questions which are bound to arise whenever we experience the final moments of a play or the last few pages of a book.

However, different types of literary work handle closure in significantly different ways. Sometimes the ending can seem to represent the inexorable climax or even the whole *raison d'être* of a work – the essential, key moment to which all other narrative elements are subordinated. This aspect of closure was explored by Roland Barthes, who provocatively described readers' desire for a satisfying ending as a quasi-sexual impulse. For Barthes, texts 'seduce' their readers, and the endings of certain types of texts are designed to evoke a specially heightened sort of pleasure (*jouissance*) equivalent to an orgasm.[4] The detective story and the romantic comedy film are particularly good examples of this type of extreme closure-driven narrative, though Barthes also had Sophocles' tragedy *Oedipus Tyrannus* in mind as a paradigm of a narrative that deploys 'an inexorable movement towards a final truth'. Barthes could easily have included Menander's sort of comedy in this category as well.

As Nick Lowe puts it (in his recognizably Barthesian book *The Classical Plot and the Invention of Western Narrative*), no other classical literary form 'pander[s] in such an extreme way to our narrative appetite for systemic closure, while simultaneously professing to reproduce the essential structure of real life.'[5] As in *The Pleasure of the Text*, a suggestive analogy is employed to explain how this process works. According to Lowe, a play by Menander is very like a game of chess: its plot rigidly adheres to 'rules' (in the shape of generic conventions); its characters can be seen as 'players' whose actions represent 'moves'; the players' goals can all broadly be understood as forms of ownership (of money, property, women or knowledge); and what happens in the last act is analogous to the 'endgame'. In Menander's formulaic, plot-driven universe, our attention is relentlessly focused on the endgame, and the conditions that must be satisfied in order for closure to be achieved include the celebration of marriage, the reconciliation of family members, the legitimation of offspring, and the continued stability of the household.[6]

All these conditions are met by the conclusion of *Samia* (and, as far as we can tell, all other comedies by Menander, Plautus and Terence). So is this the same thing as saying that the play ends happily? That is, to put it in the simplest terms, what most ordinary spectators or readers would expect of a comedy – an ending that leaves them (not just the characters in the play) feeling happy as they go home from the theatre or close the book. But people can feel happy for all sorts of different reasons, and the happiness associated with a happy ending is hard to pin down exactly. Perhaps the weddings and celebrations with which many comedies end make us happy by evoking thoughts or memories of similar events in our own lives. Perhaps the formal neatness of the plot construction gives us a sort of intellectual satisfaction, in much the same way as a completed crossword puzzle or a correctly solved algebraic equation. Perhaps the effect of a comic ending can be linked to psychological theories of humour involving the release of tension, as at the punchline of a joke.[7] Or perhaps there is more at stake than purely emotional or psychological factors. In the view of Northrop Frye, 'Comedy normally moves towards a happy ending, and the normal response of the audience to such an ending is "this should be", which sounds like a moral judgement. So it is, except that it is not moral in the restricted sense, but *social*.'[8] In other words, a 'happy' ending may also be a confirmation of our existing beliefs about social and political structures – a reaffirmation of our sense that all is right with the world.

All these considerations need to be kept in mind as we move through the final act of *Samia*. It might seem to satisfy all the criteria for a happy ending, but this is not to say that it removes every niggling anxiety or solves every problem that the plot has brought to light. In some ways it could seem to be an 'open' rather than a fully 'closed' ending. Many problematic aspects of the situation, as highlighted in the preceding acts (such as the conduct of the awful Moschion, the feelings and experiences of the female characters, the treatment of sexual relationships, the implication that married life is a dismal state, or the exposure of the worrying fragility of friendship and family ties), remain equally problematic. Menander's characters may have overcome their temporary difficulties, but the play's ending does nothing to address the more fundamental flaws in society or human nature that caused those difficulties in the first place. No doubt many of Menander's original audience members did go home with broad smiles on their faces, thinking 'this should be'; but I suspect there will have been one or two frowning faces among the crowd.

*

[V.1: *Moschion alone*] *Moschion returns to the stage and delivers yet another monologue to the audience. Having reflected on the situation, he has become angry with Demeas for suspecting him of wrongdoing; he has decided to punish his father by pretending to leave Athens and serve as a mercenary soldier in Bactria or Caria (616–40).*

Moschion's egotism

Fittingly, Moschion's opening word is the first-person pronoun *egō* – '*I* felt pleased when I was freed of the false accusation made against me . . .' (616–17). (In fact, *egō* is also his final word at the end of Act V (733) – a nice example of ring-composition for any spectator observant enough to notice it!) As we have had plenty of opportunity to observe, Moschion is a young man who thinks a good deal about his own status, feelings and privileges. He now informs us that in his absence from the stage he has experienced a change of mind and reached some important conclusions. Maybe we will be expecting him to draw some sort of improving moral lesson from everything that has happened, or to announce that he will henceforth change his behaviour: this is the sort of ethical transformation that Menander's characters do sometimes undergo towards the end of a play.[9] But no – what Moschion has decided is that Demeas has treated him badly by presuming to doubt the purity of his character; in his opinion it is Demeas who must be taught a lesson.

This lesson will take the form of a further deception: Moschion will pretend to leave Athens and travel to some far-flung region like Caria or Bactria to serve as a mercenary (628–9). On one level this is funny because, like the stock comic figure of the soldier, it is an old comic cliché. Running off to join the army is just the sort of thing that a silly young man in a comedy *would* do.[10] Incidentally the details of Moschion's ruse have been seen as another possible hint at the play's date, since many Greeks were indeed serving as mercenaries in Macedonian campaigns in Caria *c.* 315–313 BCE, so it may be that this is a rare topical allusion intended to give an added edge to the humour.[11] In any case, it is a transparently ludicrous plan, which will almost inevitably backfire on its deviser and make him a laughing stock (as Moschion himself belatedly realizes at 682–6).[12] But on the whole Moschion's plan is more disturbing than funny. What it reveals about his attitude to Demeas seems to show him up in an even worse light than ever (635–8):

> By pretending to go away I want to scare him, if nothing else. When he sees that I am not taking this lightly, he will take more care in future not to be mindless of my needs.

This attitude is particularly appalling because we have seen that Demeas is *not* mindless of Moschion's needs – far from it. He repeatedly goes out of his way to please his adopted son, even at considerable cost to himself, and to ignore his faults, even when they are staring him in the face. We are very well aware of this, because we have heard Demeas explicitly saying so earlier in the play (his remarks at 269–79 and

328–352 are particularly important in this respect). But Moschion was not present to hear these remarks; he obviously doesn't know his father well enough, nor does he fully appreciate the extent of his father's love for him. Even when, towards the end of Act V (694–713), Demeas reassures Moschion that he loves him and tries to repair their relationship by asking for his forgiveness, Moschion barely responds, except to criticize Demeas for excessive 'moralizing' (725).

A number of critics have convincingly argued that the central focus of *Samia* is the father–son relationship (rather than, as one might have expected, the love affair of Moschion and Plangon or the relationship of Demeas and Chrysis).[13] If this is true, we might expect the play to end by reaffirming the *status quo ante* described by Moschion in his prologue speech – that is, an apparently happy, functional, mutually loving relationship. But is this really what we are witnessing in these final scenes? Some readers have thought so.[14] However, the majority of recent critics and commentators (rightly, in my view) have been struck by the pettiness and immaturity of Moschion at this crucial moment of supposed reconciliation.[15] It is obvious that Moschion has not learned anything or developed in any way from his experiences. From the beginning to the end of the play he remains exactly the same: a silly, selfish egotist, concerned only with his own feelings and what other people think of him. The faults do not lie entirely on Moschion's side, of course; it may be thought that the problems in their relationship result from the failure of both father and son to communicate properly with one another.[16] But it is hard not to agree with those who see this central relationship as inherently dysfunctional, striking a discordant note, perhaps, in the play's supposedly happy ending.

Dearest Plangon

Moschion's monologue, as usual, is directed toward the audience, but in the middle of it he directly addresses his sweetheart as if she were standing right before him. 'Dearest Plangon,' he says. 'It's because of you that I shan't really do anything *andreion* ['brave' or 'manly'] – it's impossible! Love, the lord of my heart, won't allow it!' (630–2). As the commentators note, Moschion's hifalutin language here (which would not be out of place in tragedy) makes him sound rather pompous, while his mention of bravery or manliness seems to underline how puny and pusillanimous he really is.

But the most striking feature here is the phrase 'dearest Plangon' (*Plangōn philtatē*). Apostrophe to absent characters, gods, inanimate objects (and so on) is a relatively common feature in Greek drama, and would not normally seem remarkable; but its use here inevitably draws our attention to the odd fact that Plangon has never appeared on stage. She is, in a sense, one of the main characters in *Samia*, but she is given no personality, presence or voice.[17] At least she is given a name, unlike certain other young women in comedy (such as Knemon's daughter in *Dyskolos*), but this does not mean that she has any real identity as a person. She exists merely as the object of Moschion's desire and as a female who is eligible to marry and produce citizen offspring. Plangon's only appearance is in the final few moments of the play, where she is brought on stage for the marriage ceremony, but even then she is a mute character, silently handed over to her bridegroom by Nikeratos. This means that we never see events from her perspective.

But none of this is really very odd, since it corresponds in every respect to the presentation of other young women in ancient comedy.[18] Menander has no interest in what Plangon or other young women may have thought or felt about their situation, but it would be anachronistic to expect him to do so. It is easy for modern audiences to criticize ancient Greek men for their attitude towards women, and it is easy to regard Moschion in a pejorative light (whether or not we call him a rapist). But by the standards of fourth-century Athenians it may be that Moschion, for all his faults, is not a wholly objectionable figure. The fact that Moschion calls Plangon 'dearest' and talks explicitly about the power of love (*erōs*) is probably meant to soften or redeem him to some extent. It certainly provides a contrast with Moschion's earlier descriptions of the relationship, in which no mention whatsoever was made of his emotions. Indeed, the play has even been seen as promoting an idealistic and positive view of marriage based on true love (even if it is not reciprocal love).[19]

*

[V.2: *Moschion, Parmenon*] *Parmenon reappears and, apparently oblivious to the presence of his young master, delivers a monologue justifying his own actions. Moschion summons him and orders him to bring him a cloak, sword and belt for his supposed new career as a soldier. When Parmenon returns without these items and tries to explain to Moschion that the wedding is going ahead, thus rendering his plan unnecessary, Moschion punches him in the face. Parmenon goes inside again to fetch Moschion's equipment (641–90).*

Play-acting, dressing up and identity

Menander's comedies contain many moments which are metatheatrical – that is, which self-consciously draw our attention to the fact that the play we are watching is a play. The term covers a number of related phenomena (some of which we have seen earlier in *Samia*), such as direct address to the audience, use of tragic parody or allusion, reference to comic conventions, explicit reference to the actors, masks or stage machinery, and similar effects.[20] Such moments seem designed to make us reflect on the nature of the theatrical illusion or the relationship between fiction and real life, though there may be other factors at stake in each individual case. What we are seeing in this scene is a specific variety of metatheatricality sometimes called *mise en abyme*: this term is used to denote places where a character in a fictional work is seen as inventing their own fictional scenario (or 'play-within-a-play') and acting out a make-believe role.[21] Even when there is no explicit 'breaking of the illusion', it seems clear that such scenes represent some form of implicit commentary on acting a part, dressing up, improvisation or the whole art of make-believe.

We know that Moschion's proposal to become a mercenary soldier is a fiction because Moschion himself has told us so, and now we watch while the actor performs a quick costume change in front of us, replacing his costume with the military cloak (*chlamys*) and sword-belt that Parmenon brings him (686–9). Shortly afterwards Demeas enters the stage, catches sight of Moschion and immediately exclaims: 'Oh! What's this? Your costume – what does it mean?' (692). We could read this as a self-referential joke based on the semiotic function of theatrical costume.

Along with the standardized system of masks (see pp. 14–21), the costume and props used in fourth-century comic productions were conventional and stereotypical. These items generally seem to have resembled the sort of clothes and accoutrements that real-life Athenians of the period might have worn, but realism was only a secondary consideration. More importantly, they functioned as visual signs or symbols, allowing spectators to make instantaneous associations between costume, mask and character type.[22] The *chlamys* (a cloak fastened with a brooch at the shoulder) and the sword-belt, along with the light cap (*pilos*), were recurrently used as symbols denoting the 'soldier' character type.[23] This means that confusion inevitably results when Moschion – who already has his own mask and costume – adopts these quite different symbols. The mask is the same as before, but the costume and props are wrong: there is a fundamental mismatch. Demeas, as we see in other scenes, does not know his adopted son nearly as well as he believes. And now he is confronted by visual evidence that seems to indicate that he has misunderstood his son's basic character type. In other words, the metatheatrical humour here is tied up with deeper ethical concerns. Menander is not just having fun by playing around with the contrast between reality and illusion; he is connecting the theme of play-acting to the fundamental question of how well we really know or understand any other person's character.

*

[V.3: *Moschion, Parmenon, Demeas*] *Demeas sees Moschion dressed as a soldier and is shocked. Parmenon goes inside as if to bid farewell to the household before joining his master on campaign. Demeas apologizes to Moschion and admits his mistakes (690–712).*

Who are Demeas' enemies?

'I made a mistake!' Demeas admits this not once but three times in his speech to Moschion (703, 704, 707). Of course, making mistakes is what everyone does in Menander's comedies, but Demeas' unusually explicit language – and, especially, his laboured repetition of the Greek noun *hamartia* (or the related verb *hamartanō*) – has been seen as another allusion to Aristotelian thought. The concept of *hamartia* ('human error') is a central strand both in the *Poetics* (with reference to tragic characters and their fatal mistakes) and in the *Nicomachean Ethics* (with reference to ethical errors or lapses in behaviour in real life).[24] Perhaps Demeas is to be seen as viewing his behaviour through a Peripatetic lens and thus reaching a new level of self-knowledge.[25] Or perhaps he is a comic version of a tragic hero, using inflated language to bestow an extra level of dignity or mock-grandeur on his situation.[26] As elsewhere, it is up to us how seriously to take it all. But there is another incongruous detail in his speech that may help us to decide. When Demeas is reminding Moschion of his former false suspicions, he says: 'at least I didn't bring them out into the open for my enemies to laugh at' (706). This seems slightly bizarre, even paranoid. Who are these unnamed enemies? Why do we not hear about them anywhere else in the play? These questions cannot be definitively answered. However, it is probable that no such people really exist. This vaguely sinister reference is surely meant to be a joke, emphasizing Demeas' excessively 'tragic' sense of the significance of his affairs. Imagining one's enemies malevolently laughing at one's misfortunes is just what characters in tragedy do.[27]

*

[V.4: *Moschion, Demeas, Nikeratos, Plangon, mute extras*] *Nikeratos emerges from the house, sees Moschion and leaps to the conclusion that*

Moschion is running away to escape his responsibilities towards Plangon. He threatens to tie up Moschion, and is surprised when Moschion offers no resistance. Demeas tells Nikeratos to bring Plangon outside at once so that the wedding can finally take place (713–37).

Fast-forward to the end

From this point onwards the tempo of the plot suddenly increases at an astonishing rate. At lines 717–18 Nikeratos is angrily confronting his daughter's seducer, at lines 721–2 Moschion drops his sword after putting up a minimal show of resistance ... and just fifteen lines later the play has finished and the actors are taking a bow. The celebration of the long-anticipated wedding is rushed through in an oddly perfunctory manner: it comes across like a radically abridged version of a much longer scene. Even though by this point it is clear how events must inevitably conclude, it is disconcerting to see the action speeding up in this way.

As so often, when we see a feature of his drama that strikes us as puzzling, we could assume that Menander was having an off day. Maybe he had simply become bored with the whole situation now that he had finished working out the plot. Evidently ancient readers sometimes made the same sort of assumption – as is shown by the often-repeated anecdote about a friend of Menander who enquired, as the Dionysia was approaching, whether the poet had finished writing his latest play in time. 'Yes indeed,' Menander replied, 'I have finished my comedy. The plot has been worked out; I just have to write the words to go with it.'[28] Did the basic structure of his plots really matter to Menander more than their detailed execution? Perhaps there is another, more satisfying explanation for what is happening here. We could choose to see Menander as ironically underplaying the significance of the wedding by pretending that it barely matters at all. As the culmination of the colossally protracted build-up that this longed-for union has received, it is funny precisely because it is so inadequate. In other words, this is the play's final example of 'the comedy of disappointment'. Furthermore, it also functions as yet another knowing wink in the direction of the audience, who have seen so many comedies that they don't even need to watch the final scene to know where this is all heading. We all know perfectly well (Menander is implying) how these closural formulas and conventions work – so why waste time? This self-consciousness is surely deliberate: it is all part of the fun of the happy ending. We do not have enough complete extant Greek comedies to know whether this sort of *accelerando* effect was very common, but it would later be taken to extremes by Roman comedians. (Compare, for instance, the ending of Plautus' *Casina*, where Chalinus simply turns to the audience and summarizes the end of the plot, as if Plautus can't even be bothered to go through the motions of dramatizing what everyone knows is going to happen anyway.[29])

Another explanation for the change in tempo is that speeding up the action can be funny in its own right. This general principle was recognized and exploited by pioneers of film comedy in the early twentieth century, who discovered (largely by accident) that people doing things on film always look sillier if the film is played at a faster speed. The technique is particularly associated with the Keystone Cops, Buster Keaton and Charlie Chaplin, but it is widely encountered in silent cinema of the 1910s and 1920s.[30] Perhaps this analogy from cinema may help us to appreciate the effect of the last scene of *Samia*. What seems to be happening in each medium is roughly the same: the increased rapidity of action and movement leads to a decreased sense of reality or credibility. We are more than ever made aware of the extreme artificiality of the events on stage or screen – which may colour our response to the characters and their situation in other ways. In the words of Eric Bentley (whose discussion of silent cinema in *The Life of Drama* contains many suggestive points of contact), 'the speeding-up of movement in the typical silent movie farces had a definite psychological and moral effect, namely, of making actions seem abstract and automatic when in life they would be concrete and subject to free will.'[31]

Comedy as 'evidence'

The play's final scene, together with certain features that have been mentioned in passing during the preceding acts, gives us a very detailed account of Moschion and Plangon's wedding – including the preliminary arrangements, the domestic preparations for the celebratory feast, the accompanying rituals and the ceremony itself. For this reason *Samia* is often cited in historical studies of the classical Greek wedding.[32]

Nowadays Menander's readers tend to fall into two categories: those who are mainly interested in theatre and want to appreciate the plays as works of art for their own sake, and those who treat the plays as a source of evidence for Athenian social history. (Of course there is a certain amount of overlap between these groups.) Both types of reader are likely to run into difficulties sooner or later. But the social historians have a harder job than the literary critics, because the direct evidential value of poetry, drama and other types of imaginative literature is questionable. Whatever we think Menander's aims were, it is clear that he did not write his plays with the express purpose of providing future historians with factual data about his life and times.

Eric Griffiths, in an illuminating general discussion of the problems of reading literature as 'evidence', writes: 'When we read fictions, we are not concerned primarily or even at all with whether what they say is true or not . . . Literature's testimony to the world beyond literature is at best oblique and stylized.'[33] Griffiths is principally concerned with modern European literature, but his remarks are more widely applicable. No matter what type of literature we are dealing with, we need to appreciate the precise degree of 'obliquity' and the exact way in which reality has been 'stylized' – which means that we have to be finely attuned to the conventions of each literary genre as well as the historical context. In fact, as Griffiths goes on to show, the distinction between 'literature' and other 'non-literary' texts is largely irrelevant. Every single written document – including a law-court speech, a historical work in prose, or even a list – is a text that needs to be processed, decoded and interpreted according to its own rules: no text is ever just an assemblage of factual data.

These considerations arise whenever we read any ancient text,[34] but comedy's relationship to the real world can often seem especially oblique. Even a comedian such as Menander, who was famed for his supposed realism, is not simply depicting the world as it is.[35] His plays may not be as fantastic as those of Aristophanes, but they contain much that is self-evidently silly, stylized, exaggerated or absurd. Their settings do not represent a true reflection of Athenian society so much as a distortion or refraction.

It cannot automatically be taken for granted, then, that Menander's depiction of weddings is more realistic than his treatment of other aspects of sexual relationships. Take, for example, the presentation of the theme of rape in *Samia* and elsewhere. Are the plots of these plays representative of everyday Athenian life and normative cultural attitudes? If so, we might conclude that rape was a frequent occurrence; that Athenians didn't consider rape to be a terribly serious crime; that rape invariably resulted in pregnancy; that rapists always married their victims, and that this was seen as a cause for celebration. Somehow one doubts that this was really the case,[36] but the problem is that we do not have sufficient historical source material apart from the plays themselves to confirm or deny the impression that the comedians give us.

Just imagine if the main evidence for social attitudes to murder in twenty-first-century British society consisted of a few episodes of the popular television show *Midsomer Murders*.[37] If historians a couple of millennia from now were to take this evidence at face value, they might conclude that murder was commonplace in English villages; that ordinary citizens showed no discernible surprise or terror when faced with murder; that murderers always killed more than one victim at a time; that bizarre and grotesque methods were invariably employed; that all cases of homicide were investigated by just two police detectives; that every murderer was brought to justice after admitting their guilt – and so on. Because we happen to have other sources of knowledge, we are able to see that as 'evidence' *Midsomer Murders* is seriously defective.

Yet this show (though somewhat larky and tongue-in-cheek) is not even a comedy: it is a drama series in the realist tradition.

Caveats must be carefully applied before treating Moschion and Plangon's wedding as typical of Athenian weddings in general. Since most of its details are paralleled in other literary and artistic sources, and since the wedding itself is apparently not a target of humour, we can be reasonably confident that the events described or depicted here do have some verisimilitude. But still we need to acknowledge the crucial problem of methodological circularity facing anyone, historian and literary critic alike, who attempts to interpret the plays of Menander. The shortage of external source material for the historical context means that these texts have to be explained *by reference to themselves*: they are treated simultaneously as 'evidence' and as unique literary works that have to be interpreted in the light of that 'evidence'. This basic problem, sometimes referred to as the 'hermeneutic circle', also bedevils the study of many other classical Greek authors.

And so we return to the wedding itself. In the previous acts various references have already been made to the wedding preparations and preliminary rituals, all of which are narrated, as if taking place inside the house, rather than physically shown on stage.

In Act I Parmenon tells Chrysis that Moschion is preparing to sacrifice, put on a garland and cut up the wedding cake (74–5).

During Act II Moschion is extremely eager to push on with the wedding rituals. At 123–5 he himself apparently describes how he has already made sacrifice, invited friends to the wedding feast, sent slaves to fetch water for the bride and groom's ritual bath, shared out the cake, and sung the traditional wedding song (*hymenaios*) – though it turns out that he was just daydreaming. A little later, at 156–9, he urges Demeas to let him go inside and bathe, pour libations and place incense on the altar, but Demeas makes it clear that they must wait for Nikeratos to give his permission.

Much is made, in Act III, of the cook and his attendants getting ready to cook the celebratory meal (282–95, 356–89) and of the bride's father preparing the sheep for sacrifice (399–404).

In Act IV, Demeas makes another reference to the *hymenaios*, saying that he will force himself to sing it even if unwilling (449); later he tells Nikeratos to get on with the burning of incense (609).

Earlier in Act V the burning of incense is mentioned yet again by Parmenon, but this time it is clear that it actually is happening rather than just being talked about in prospect. Parmenon also reports that wine is being mixed for a libation, and that the unfortunate sheep from Act III has been killed and is cooking on the fire (673–4).

From all these scattered references we can piece together a composite picture of the paraphernalia of the marriage ceremony. Nevertheless, it does not give us a complete picture. In exactly what order did these events take place, and did it matter? Did both families perform sacrifices and libations? Which gods were involved? How much incense was burned, and when, and by whom? Who exactly sang the *hymenaios*? We have to look to other sources to find an answer to these questions.

But finally we come to the moment at which the silent Plangon emerges from the house, escorted by Nikeratos, and is formally handed over to her new husband (725–9). This solemn ceremony, known as *engyēsis*, marks the symbolic transfer of the woman from one household to the other, and is legally binding. The fact that it features in almost identical form in several other comedies, with the same form of words being used in each case, strongly suggests that this can be treated as an accurate and realistic portrayal of the main part of the wedding.[38]

> **Nikeratos** [*to Plangon*] Come over here, please. [*to Moschion*] In front of witnesses I give you this woman to have as your wife, to raise a crop of legitimate children; I also give you, as a dowry, all my property – when I die, that is, which God forfend; I hope that I shall live for ever!
>
> **Moschion** I have her, I take her, I cherish her.

Even though this is obviously a standard formula, the reference to 'a crop of legitimate children' is bound to strike us as incongruous or ironical in the circumstances. Furthermore, Nikeratos' simultaneous giving and withholding of the dowry – normally a requirement of the marriage contract – is an odd gesture. As the commentators point out, this could be a way of paying Moschion back for his bad behaviour, since as a self-confessed seducer of a free woman he could have expected a far worse punishment, or it could simply be that Nikeratos is being characterized as too poor or mean to offer what would be expected of a typical father-in-law.

Bathtime – and applause

'One thing remains to be done,' announces Demeas. 'Someone needs to fetch the water for bathing' (729–30). As we have seen, the characters have already made plenty of references to this ritual bath, which (so it seems) would normally precede the other parts of the ceremony.[39] Demeas' anxiety that the nuptial bath should happen now, even if it is out of sequence, may reflect the belief that it was an indispensable part of the ritual. Or perhaps it is simply a pretext for Demeas to turn back to the door of his house and call on Chrysis – together with the other women of the household, the water-bearer, a musician, and others bearing torches and garlands – to come and join in the wedding celebrations (730–3).

Does the stage now fill up with people as the comedy comes to a close? As usual, the absence of stage directions in the text makes it hard to be certain what happens here, so we have to use our imagination to fill in the gaps. Nevertheless, the fact that Demeas explicitly mentions all these individuals in turn, together with the fact that Moschion starts to put on the garlands that someone has brought in (732–3), suggests that these people are indeed visible to the audience. The on-stage presence of a large number of 'extras', accompanied by music and other general hubbub, would create a party atmosphere befitting the occasion. The reappearance of Chrysis and (perhaps) other characters from earlier in the play, such as the cook and the nurse, all of them played by mute actors wearing the appropriate masks and costumes, would also have something of the valedictory feel of a 'curtain call'. (It would be interesting to know whether that other highly important mute character, the baby, also appeared in this montage. Plangon would not have been nursing him during her own marriage ceremony, which may imply that Chrysis is still holding him in her arms, as ever: this would be a nice touch.) A celebration in which everyone was seen to be participating would create a sense of inclusion, reconciliation and completeness – which would no doubt help to smooth over any remaining problems and encourage the spectators to forget temporarily about any lingering unease.

And now it is time for us to bid the characters farewell and return to real life. The very last words, as so often in Greek and Roman comedy, dissolve the dramatic illusion once and for all, explicitly signalling to us that the world of the play has ceased to exist. Demeas, who delivers the final lines (733–7), is no longer speaking as Demeas but instead adopts the persona of Menander himself:

> Beautiful boys, young men, old men, gentlemen of the audience – all together now, give us your enthusiastic applause as a sign of your goodwill and a welcome offering to the god of the theatre! And may the immortal goddess Nike, who sits beside Dionysus at this, the finest of contests, accompany my performers for ever more!

This is not the first time that the presence of the spectators has been directly acknowledged, but it is the most important by far. This time we are being called upon to participate actively in the drama – for our contribution is now absolutely vital. The noise of our clapping, laughing, whistling, cheering and stamping of feet is a sound effect that can be seen as an intrinsic component of the performance. Indeed, just as much as any other feature mentioned in the script, audience applause is an essential condition of the happy ending. A comedy that ended in silence would be a disaster.

These lines, with their call to interactive engagement, are vivid and memorable, but they were not written specially for *Samia*: they are variations on a conventional formula. Closely similar expressions are found in all the other comedies of Menander where the ending survives

(*Dyskolos*, *Misoumenos*, *Sikyonios*), and it may be that every comedy of the period ended in more or less the same way.[40] The literal meaning of the lines is important – we are being reminded that the festival is a competitive event, and that the warmth of our response may influence the judges in their award of the prizes – but the symbolic and functional meaning is equally important (or more so). The formula is a formal signal of closure, immediately recognized as such. Like the lowering of a curtain, a recapitulation of the signature tune, a plagal 'Amen', or the appearance of that familiar two-word caption in enormous letters during the final frames of the film credits, it tells us that this is THE END.

[illegible]

THE END.

Notes

Introduction

1 Pickard-Cambridge 1988: 135–6.
2 This approach is taken from Josipovici 2016, a compelling study of *Hamlet* which has hugely influenced my own work. See esp. p. 9: 'How, at a practical level, to marry discussion of what the play is "about", the kind of discussion that forms the staple of literary criticism, with discussion of how the play unfolds in time? The trouble with undue emphasis on the former is that the unfolding aspect is lost; the trouble with the latter is that it can descend into mere commentary and paraphrase . . . and lose sight of the play's deeper meanings.' Sutherland 2005 has also been a model and source of inspiration.
3 For the sources see *Poetae Comici Graeci* (K-A) VI.2, pp. 1–43; for discussion see Arnott 1979: xiii–xix; Sommerstein 2013: 1–4.
4 See Nervegna 2013.
5 Lefkowitz 2012: 109–12.
6 *Suda* M 580; [Anon.] *On Comedy* [*Prolegomena on Comedy* III, p. 10 Koster]; Aulus Gellius 17.4.4; Anaxandrides Test. 1–2 K-A; Alexis Test. 1 K-A.
7 Nervegna 2013: 137.
8 Sidwell 2000, Csapo 2000, Wright 2013, etc.
9 See the 'Guide to Further Reading', p. 149–50.
10 Lape 2004: 1–10 is a useful guide to the political context.
11 See Major 1997.
12 For the most recent discussion see Sommerstein 2013: 44–6. On the topical allusions, see below, pp. 98–100, 117.
13 See now Csapo and Wilson 2020.
14 A few smaller papyrus finds and other fragments also exist. See Arnott 1979: xxvi–xxx for a brief introduction to the 'rebirth' of Menander via papyri.
15 Lefebvre 1907.
16 Kasser and Austin 1969.

17 See Porter 2006 on the complexities inherent in the concept of 'classics'.

18 www.apgrd.ox.ac.uk (accessed 9th April 2020).

19 See pp. 24–7.

20 Zagagi 1994 is a good discussion of this aspect of Menander.

Chapter 1

1 Pickard-Cambridge 1988: 263.

2 Audiences' noisy behaviour, eating and drinking: see Aeschines, *Against Ctesiphon* 76, Demosthenes, *Against Meidias* 226, Aristotle, *Nicomachean Ethics* 1175b, Athenaeus, *Deipnosophistae* 11.464, Plato, *Laws* 700c–701a, Theophrastus, *Characters* 11.3.

3 Cf. Cicero, *Tusculan Disputations* 4.63 on the inaudible opening lines of Euripides' *Orestes* (which Socrates demanded to be repeated).

4 On textual problems and conjectural reconstruction see Sommerstein 2013 and other commentaries. Images of the entire papyrus are available on the BodmerLab website (labelled 'Papyri PB M'): see https://bodmerlab.unige.ch/fr/constellations/papyri (accessed 6th April 2020).

5 Hytner 2017: 8.

6 An author might, however, play on the fact that in Greek *prosōpon* can mean 'face' or 'mask' (e.g. *Dyskolos* 111).

7 Wiles 2007, esp. 1–13.

8 See Webster, Green and Seeberg 1995: 2–3 (citing other authorities for the rule).

9 Pollux, *Onomasticon* 4.143–54: text, translation and discussion in Webster, Green and Seeberg 1995: 6–51.

10 For a range of approaches see Webster 1970: 73–96, MacCary 1970, Brown 1987, Pickard-Cambridge 1988: 177–231, Wiles 1991, Marshall 2006: 129–32, Petrides 2014.

11 Bernabò Brea 1992–3.

12 Poe 1996.

13 See, however, pp. 71–2 on the cook's mask.

14 For the view that masks have strong significatory properties, and attempts to interpret them in the light of Hellenistic theories of physiognomy, see Wiles 1991: 150–87; Petrides 2014: 142–51.

15 MacCary 1970.

16 This is shown conclusively by Brown 1987.

17 Cf. Arnott 1979: xxxii, Zagagi 1994: 45.

18 See Sommerstein 2010 on titling conventions.

19 On Menander's prologues see Holzberg 1974: 6–100, Ireland 1981; cf. Sharrock 2009: 22–95 on the more exuberant prologues of Roman comedy.

20 Cf. (from *Samia*) 216, 328–9, 446–8, 683, 726, 733–7. On the convention see Bain 1977: 186–207.

21 This interpretation of *Samia* 13 depends on a conjectural emendation: see Sommerstein 2013: 104–5. (I translate Sommerstein's text here, not Arnott's.)

22 For analysis of this and other scenes from *Samia* in relation to rhetoric and the law, see Scafuro 1997: 238–78; Carey 2013: 94–5. Cf. pp. 66–7, 94–8.

23 See Hall 1995.

24 Barigazzi 1965; Cinaglia 2012 and 2014; Casanova 2014.

25 Different interpretations are offered by Mette 1969 (wholly positive, emphasizing M's civic virtue); Jacques 2003: xxx–xxxi (largely positive); Blume 1974: 11–12 (M's self-assessment seen as being confirmed by D's use of the same word); Blanchard 2002 (stresses the inherent ambiguity of the word and sees M as ultimately immature and superficial); Voelke 2012 (largely negative: M's concern with appearances seen as the root cause of his problems); Sommerstein 2013: 107 (M's *previous* good behaviour seen as contrasting with his more recent lapse).

26 The festival is discussed by Parker 2005: 283–8; this passage from *Samia* is one of the key pieces of evidence for historians of religion.

27 Cf. Omitowoju 2002: 199 ('There is no distinction based on whether the act was consensual or non-consensual which can have any relevance'); cf. Scafuro 1997: 259–65.

28 This subject has been widely discussed: see esp. Omitowoju 2002 (who cites and discusses many others). Omitowoju's argument that the woman's consent was *completely* irrelevant is modified by Sommerstein 2006.

29 See Adair 1997: 150–2 on the 'performative' aspects of rape as a speech act.

30 Rosivach 1998 shows how pervasive the rape motif was and discusses its many permutations as a plot device (see esp. pp. 36–7).

31 This is seen clearly by Pierce 1997.

32 See Hardwick 2000 on 'cultural translation'.
33 The real version of the quotation appears in A. Conan Doyle, *The Sign of the Four* (1890), Ch. 6.
34 The concept first appears in a letter to Alexander Semenovich Lazarev (1 November 1889), but Chekhov restated it numerous times: see Simmons 1962: 190.
35 Ireland 1983. Cf. below, pp. 107, 124, 143.
36 Capps 1910: 224–5, 237.
37 Allinson 1921: 130.
38 Körte 1932; cf. Webster 1950: 40–7 for a critique.
39 Gomme 1936: 70–2.
40 On slaves in Greek comedy see Krieter-Spiro 1997, Konstan 2013.
41 See Blume 1974: 22–3, who notes that Menander wrote a comedy called *Androgynos*. Cf. pp. 75–7 on insults.
42 Note, however, that other slaves in the play, even mute minor characters, are slow to obey orders: see *Samia* 104–5.
43 See Arnott 2010: 310–19 on the prominence of *hetaira* comedies/titles in the early fourth century; cf. Webster 1970: 22–4, 63–4; Krieter-Spiro 1997.
44 See Traill 2008: 157–8.
45 On the connotations of the word *pallakē* (normally translated 'concubine') see pp. 46–7.
46 On the baby as 'prop' and/or 'hero' in Menander see Heap 2003.
47 See (e.g.) Sandbach 1986; West 1991; Traill 2008: 162–8. For a different view cf. Dedoussi 1988.
48 Ogden 1996: 189.
49 Treu 1981; Lape 2004.
50 See Loraux 1987, esp. 7–30.
51 Menander, *Perikeiromene* 505; Philemon fr. 118 K-A.
52 Cf. Wiles 1991: 68–85 on 'binary oppositions' and semiotic approaches to character and staging.
53 Noted by Sommerstein 2013: 22.
54 On characterization by differentiated speech here see Katsouris 1975b: 106–9; cf. Gomme and Sandbach 1973: 554–5 and Sandbach 1970.
55 Cf. Blume 1974: 50–51.
56 Collard 1989 (comparing other descriptions at *Samia* 412 and 550).

57 Gomme and Sandbach 1973: 554, followed by Bain 1983, reassign 98–101 to Nikeratos (comparing *Samia* 399–420); cf. Katsouris 1975b: 108.
58 Sommerstein 2013: 136, citing *Odyssey* 12.377–83 and Aristophanes, *Clouds* 584–6.
59 Byrne 2012: 120–23.
60 See esp. Major 1997; Nervegna 2013: 11–45; Lape and Moreno 2014.
61 Even within antiquity readers complained about all the obscure references in Aristophanes: see Plutarch, *Sympotic Questions* 7.8 (*Moralia* 711f–712a).
62 See pp. 98–100.
63 Treu 1969: 241; Blume 1974: 46–7; cf. Fountoulakis 2009 for a more sceptical view.
64 Sommerstein 2013: 135.

Chapter 2

1 See Maidment 1935.
2 Aristotle, *Poetics* 1456a 27–31.
3 See (e.g.) Webster 1970: 59, Pickard-Cambridge 1988: 233–4. Gomme and Sandbach 1973: 12 are cautious about making generalizations.
4 Jackson 2020: 139–65.
5 Jackson 2020: 113–37, citing (*inter alia*) Antidotus fr. 2, Eubulus fr. 2, fr. 103; *com. adesp.* fr. 1032 K–A. Rothwell 1995 reaches similar conclusions.
6 E.g. *P.Ash.inv.* 89B 131, 33; *P.Strasb.* WG 304–7; *P.Köln* 20270–9. See Jackson 2020: 144–5.
7 See West 1992 on all aspects of Greek music.
8 Pohlmann and West 2002; www.armand-dangour.com (accessed 3 March 2020).
9 I am relying on my own memory and diary entries here, but the Oxford Archive of Performances of Greek and Roman Drama (#2821) preserves some information about this production, including the name of the choreographer (Isidoros Sideris) and composer (Michalis Christodoulidis). See http://www.apgrd.ox.ac.uk/productions/production/2821 (accessed 3 March 2020).
10 See Halliwell 2008: 390–425 on 'the fluctuating presence or absence of laughter' in Menander; cf. similar descriptions of Menander's tone in

Hurst 1990 ('chiaroscuro') and Petrides 2014: 61–2 ('bittersweet'). Cf. pp. 68–70.

11 This definition is taken from Sommerstein 2014: 14. Cf. Brown 1990: 247–50, Omitowoju 2002: 211–23 on specific terms for different categories of women in sexual relationships.

12 See Traill 2008: 156–69.

13 Konstan 1993: 142.

14 Sommerstein 2013: 210, comparing Aeschines 1.80–3, Menander fr. 472, Timocles fr. 24.

15 Cf. my earlier discussion of the significatory properties of masks: pp. 14–21.

16 Whom does Nikeratos threaten to kill at *Samia* 560–2? The text is ambiguous: see Gomme and Sandbach 1973: 607–8 and Sommerstein 2013: 273 (who prefer to see Chrysis, not Nikeratos' wife, as the victim).

17 Harding 1998: see esp. 5–6. For comparison of Menander and Jane Austen cf. Green 1990: 74.

18 Ogden 1996: 203–5 (comparing Euripides, *Andromache* 638, F141, F168 and other passages). See also pp. 33–4 on citizenship and legitimacy as preoccupations of Menander.

19 The others (*Samia* 163–5, 206–9, 340–2) are all spoken by Demeas.

20 On quotable maxims in Menander (and comedy more generally) see Wright forthcoming.

21 See Liapis 2002.

22 See Cusset and Lhostis 2011; cf. Wright forthcoming.

23 Aristotle (*Rhetoric* 1395a2–7) regards old men as best qualified to use *gnōmai* in speeches.

24 Bain 1983: xix.

25 Nervegna 2013: 203–20.

26 See Vogt-Spira 1992 for detailed discussion; cf. briefer remarks in Zagagi 1994: 143–7.

27 Vogt-Spira 1992: 146–67.

28 Aristotle, *Nicomachean Ethics* 1100b8–30; *Physics* 2.4.6; Demetrius, *Peri Tychēs* (*FGrHist* IIb 228.39, quoted by Polybius 29.21); Theophrastus, *Callisthenes* (fr. 493, quoted by Cicero, *Tusculan Disputations* 5.24; Plutarch *On Fortune* 97).

29 See e.g. Barigazzi 1965; Casanova 2014.

30 Cinaglia 2015, esp. 102–46 on chance.

31 Cinaglia 2015: 103.

32 See Parker 1996: 227–37 on the cult; cf. Parker 2005: 136–52 on comic religion and ritual generally (though he has little to say about fourth-century comedy).

33 Rutherford 2012: 157 supplies useful references.

34 On Menander and tragedy see Gutzwiller 2000; Cusset 2003; Petrides 2014; cf. pp. 78–81, 92–3, 108–11.

35 See Wiles 2000: 113–14 on the aesthetics of outdoor theatre and the audience's awareness of the natural landscape.

36 On the possible use of scene-painting (*skēnographia*) in the Greek theatre, see Small 2013. Wiles 1991: 45 assumes the use of contrasting painted panels by each doorway; cf. Wiles 1997: 161–2 (with ref. to fifth-century tragedy).

37 Frost 1988: 105–6.

38 See Frost 1988: 102–17 on entrances/exits, and esp. 6–7 on the noise of the door (e.g. *Samia* 300–1, 366, 532, 555, 567, 669). Cf. Wiles 2000: 118 on the semiotics of inside versus outside in performance.

39 On this distinction see Issacharoff 1981.

40 This unanswerable question is a perennial problem for scholars: see Henderson 1991.

41 For discussion of the text and restoration see Arnott 2000: 62; Sommerstein 2013: 166.

42 Frost 1988: 7–8.

43 Cf. pp. 34–5, on Moschion's suicide threat.

44 See Duckworth 1994: 281–5.

45 E.g. Anaxandrides frs. 53, 57; Antiphanes frs. 270, 285; Diodorus fr. 3; Diphilus fr. 114; Menander frs. 236, 374, 508, 804; Philemon frs. 120, 165, 167; Philippides fr. 6; Philiscus fr. 1; Theophilus fr. 6; Plautus, *Aulularia* 139–40, *Casina* 227, *Epidicus* 180.

Chapter 3

1 See Blundell 1980 on Menander's monologues.

2 See esp. Bain 1977 on the use of such conventions; cf. Marshall 2006: 159–202 (with reference to Roman drama).

3 On rhetoric, monologues and narrative in tragedy see Goward 1999.
4 See pp. 78–81; cf. pp. 54–5, 92–3, 108–11.
5 Nünlist 2002 discusses this convention and supplies a list of references (254–60).
6 Munteanu 2002; Cinaglia 2012. For Aristotle's definition of *anagnōrisis* see *Poetics* 11.1452a29–31.
7 Carey 2013; cf. Scafuro 2003 and 1997: 259–63.
8 Carey 2013: 94.
9 Hamilton 1932; cf. Tarn 1952: 273 (describing Menander as 'the dreariest desert in literature'). More recent scholarship, though more nuanced, tends to adapt either a scathing or an apologetic tone: see e.g. Green 1990: 67–79.
10 Arnott 1997, esp. 65–6. Arnott also claims that Menander's humour is closer to 'modern TV situation-comedies' (which ones?), but he does not elaborate on this claim.
11 Halliwell 2008: 390–425. See also Griffiths 2018: 82–3 on the distinction between laughter and other valid 'expressions of a comic sense'.
12 See Willi 2002: 1–30 for a helpful outline of Menander's language, including bibliographic guidance; cf. Katsouris 1975b on language as a means of characterization.
13 See Sommerstein 2013: 190, citing Menander, *Dyskolos* 292–3, 398–9, 410, Alexis fr. 177, Anaxippus fr. 1, Hegisippus fr. 1, Sosipater fr. 1.
14 Kawin 1972; cf. p. 38 on the 'callback' technique.
15 E.g. *Frogs* 1–14, *Wasps* 60–1, *Peace* 741–3; discussed by Wright 2012: 90–102.
16 Cf. other entrances marking changes of mood and pace: e.g. Parmenon at 61–2; Demeas and Nikeratos at 96 (discussed above, pp. 30–1, 36–7).
17 Webster 1970: 65–6, 116, 128–9, 158–9; Nesselrath 1990: 297–309; cf. Krieter-Spiro 1997.
18 Wilkins 2000.
19 See Webster, Green and Seeberg 1995: 31–2 for discussion of possible correspondences to Pollux's types 25 *and* 26.
20 Pollux, *Onomasticon* 4.143–54 (see pp. 14–21); Athenaeus, *Deipnosophistae* 14.659a ('the ancients referred to a cook with citizen status as *maisōn*, and a foreign cook as *tettix*'). See Wiles 1991: 78, 168.
21 Wiles 1991: 50 assumes that they were unmasked.

22 Cf. orders to mute extras at *Samia* 202, 321–2, 325, 440–3, 732. Bain 1981: 44–7 discusses conventions relating to masters, servants and orders in comedy, though his main interest is in tragedy.

23 Blume 1974: 34–6.

24 *Samia* 553–4, 560–2, 574–5, 581–2, 719–21.

25 Lape and Moreno 2014: 359.

26 Dickey 1996: 165–73 (quotation from 165).

27 Cf. *Aspis* 399–433, *Epitrepontes* 1123–8, etc. On tragic citation in Menander see Cusset 2003: 133–62.

28 Gutzwiller 2000: 105.

29 Cf. Hurst 1990: 101 ('Pour retrouver son bon sens, Déméas doit explicitement quitter la sphère de la tragédie').

30 See also pp. 54–5, 92–3, 108–11.

31 Katsouris 1975a, Hurst 1990, Gutzwiller 2000, Cusset 2003, Wright 2012 and 2013, Bakola, Prauscello and Telò 2013.

32 See Katsouris 1975a: 131–43, Cusset 2003: 163–8.

33 Sophocles frs 718–20 *TrGF* (Radt); Euripides frs 803a–818 *TrGF* (Kannicht); for a full account of the myth see Apollodorus 3.13.8. Tragedies on the subject were also written by Ion of Chios and Astydamas the Younger.

34 See esp. Jäkel 1982; Sommerstein 2013: 36–40.

35 Gomme and Sandbach 1973: 598 ('In the circumstances this is comic, and even if Moschion had been guilty, Nikeratos' language might be thought overdone').

36 Charitōnidēs, Kahil and Ginouvès 1970: this publication includes discussion of all the mosaics as well as high-quality images (see esp. 38–41 on the *Samia* mosaic). Subsequent discussions include Webster, Green and Seeberg 1995: 86–98; Csapo 2010: 147–58; Nervegna 2013: 137–69.

37 Halliwell 2008: 410, 425.

38 For different estimates of the date see Charitōnidēs, Kahil and Ginouvès 1970: 29–30; Berczelly 1988.

39 Csapo 1999, 2010: 153–4; Nervegna 2013: 169.

40 See Webster, Green and Seeberg 1995, esp. 93: it is pointed out that the *Samia* mosaic (XZ31) closely resembles the *Plokion* mosaic from Chania (XZ29).

41 Green 1994: 112: 'The wide accessibility of the originals of these pictures and their reproduction in such a wide range of media argues for their quasi-public standing.'

42 See Pütz 2014.
43 See Rothwell 2007.
44 Cratinus frs 39–51 K-A; see Storey 2011: I.284–95.
45 Arnott 1959: 179.

Chapter 4

1 The explanation of metre offered here is simplified down to bare essentials: for more detail see West 1987: 19–24; Gomme and Sandbach 1973: 36–9; Sommerstein 2013: 46–8.
2 'The Black Sea! Fat old men! Fish everywhere!' (*Samia* 98).
3 'Chrysis is not the mother of the baby she is now nursing' (*Samia* 695).
4 Aristotle, *Rhetoric* 3.1408b36; *Poetics* 1449a22–4.
5 Sommerstein 2013: 233. Cf. Pickard-Cambridge 1988: 164–5 on different metres and modes of delivery in drama (citing e.g. Menander, *Dyskolos* 880–958 for the use of the *aulos* to accompany iambic tetrameters).
6 Gomme and Sandbach 1973: 36–7.
7 See the Guide to Further Reading (p. 148) on translations of *Samia*.
8 On *skōr* ('shit', the root of *skatophagos*) as a primary obscenity see Henderson 1975: 26, 35–6. Menander uses *skatophagein/-os* elsewhere (*Samia* 550; *Perikeiromene* 394); cf. *Dyskolos* 461 (*kinētiān*, 'fuck'), 892 (*laikazein*, 'suck off'); *Perikeiromene* 485 (*laikastria*, 'cocksucker'); *Phasma* 17 (*chezein*, 'shit'); fr. 397 (*hypobinētiān*, 'fuck'); fr. 430 (an old man is called *muochodos*, 'mouse shit'). For obscenities in other fourth-century comic fragments cf. *CGFPR* 138.8, 219.36. See Bain 1991 for discussion.
9 Henderson 1975; Willi 2002: 10–11.
10 Henderson 1975: 29.
11 Aristotle, *Poetics* 1449b12 is the *locus classicus*. For comprehensive discussion see Schwindt 1994; cf. Germany 2014 with ref. to Menander (though he does not discuss the *Samia* passage).
12 Lowe 2007: 66–7.
13 Cf., perhaps, Sostratos' words at *Dyskolos* 187–8: 'A lot can happen in a day!'
14 On Platon's *Long Night* and Plautus' *Amphitryo* see Christenson 2000: 47–55.
15 See Zagagi 1994: 94–141 on Menander as a repository of contemporary social norms and values.

16 On Athenian law see Carey 1995.
17 Porter 1997; Scafuro 1997; cf. pp. 22–3, 64–7 on quasi-legal language in *Samia*.
18 See Sommerstein 2013: 260.
19 Cf. Scafuro 1997: 259–60.
20 Cf. Rosivach 1998: 20–1 on 'doing the right thing' in *Samia*.
21 A point well brought out by Omitowoju 2002: 200–2.
22 *Lexicon of Greek Personal Names* II.121.
23 Cf. Menander frs 55, 225, 304; Alexis frs 213, 259; Antiphanes fr. 197; Timocles fr. 9, etc.
24 Sommerstein 2013: 285.
25 Arnott 1996: 610; cf. Arnott 2000: 7–12.
26 On 'asides' and related conventions see Bain 1977 (to which my own analysis is indebted).
27 It is uncertain whether the actors in Menander's time used a raised stage and/or the *orchēstra*: see Wiles 1991: 37–9.
28 '*a*' and '*b*' are used here to indicate the first part or the second part of the verse in question.
29 Gomme and Sandbach 1973: 603 ('There is intentional bathos in the very ordinary language that follows').
30 Romero-Trillo 2013.
31 On conventions of presentation in ancient books and manuscripts of drama see Lowe 1962; on the papyri of Menander see Gomme and Sandbach 1973: 39–49.
32 But see Taplin 1977.
33 For a photograph of the page in question see https://bodmerlab.unige.ch/fr/constellations/papyri/mirador/1072205365?page=015 (accessed 31 March 2020).
34 Bader 1971, Petersmann 1971; cf. Frost 1988: 6–7.
35 See Duckworth 1994: 116–17 (supplying many useful references).
36 By my count there are forty-nine separate occasions in *Samia* on which the door opens for a character's entrance or exit. Cf. Frost 1988: 102–17.
37 Cf. *Samia* 730, where it is implied that Chrysis is supervising the female servants.
38 Ireland 1983; cf. Ireland 1994. See also pp. 28–30.
39 See Traill 2008: 167–8. Cf. West 1991: 22–3 ('for many readers the Bodmer Papyrus brought a major disappointment by ruling out the possibility that

Chrysis might be rewarded with the unexpected disclosure of citizen status and the prospect of marriage to Demeas').

40 Cf. Keuls 1973: 18.

41 For the myth see Apollodorus 1.9.6, 2.4.2–3. Cf. Aeschylus *TrGF* III p. 302 *TrGF* (Radt); Sophocles frs 60–76, 165–70, 378–83 *TrGF* (Radt); Euripides frs 316–348 *TrGF* (Kannicht).

42 Contrast Scafuro 1997: 276–8, who sees 'the intersection of myth and social reality' here as uncomfortably troubling.

43 E.g. Aristotle, *Poetics,* esp. 1449b24–8; Menander, *Epitrepontes* 1123–6; Philippides fr. 18 K-A; Nicostratus fr. 29 K–A, as well as the passage quoted. See Gutzwiller 2000, Rosen 2012, Wright 2013: 613–19.

44 Cf. pp. 35, 54–5, 78–81.

45 Cf. pp. 50–5.

Chapter 5

1 Horace, *Ars Poetica* 189 ('let your play be not longer or shorter than five acts'); see Gomme and Sandbach 1973: 19–21 and Holzberg 1974: 121–73 on Menander's handling of the five-act convention.

2 Barthes 1973; Kermode 1967; Schlueter 1995; Miller 1981.

3 On closure in ancient comedy the fundamental work is Sharrock 2009: 250–89 (with reference to Roman comedy but with wider application); cf. Dunn 1996 on tragedy.

4 Barthes 1973: 20–1.

5 Lowe 2000: 191.

6 Lowe 2000: 201–21.

7 See Weitz 2009 on Freudian and other theories of humour.

8 Frye 1957: 167.

9 Cf. *Dyskolos* 709–47, 797–819, 861–5; *Epitrepontes* 980–9, 1104–13; *Perikeiromene* 1016–22.

10 The same motif is seen in Terence, *The Self-Tormentor* (based on a Menandrean original) and Plautus, *Trinummus*; cf. soldiers in Menander's *Kolax, Misoumenos, Perikeiromene* and *Sikyonios.* See Zagagi 1994: 35–7; on comic soldiers cf. MacCary 1972.

11 Gomme and Sandbach 1973: 542–3; Arnott 2000: 10–11; Sommerstein 2013: 45–6. Cf. other real-life references in the play (see pp. 98–111).

12 Blume 1974: 251–2.
13 Mette 1969; Stoessl 1969; Grant 1986; Weissenberger 1991; Blanchard 2002.
14 E.g. Jacques 2003: xxviii; Mette 1969; Lloyd-Jones 1972.
15 E.g. Blanchard 2002: 65; Grant 1986; Stoessl 1969: 208; West 1991: 19–23; Sommerstein 2013: 288–9.
16 See Weissenberger 1991, esp. 421–4; Ireland 1994.
17 Cf. pp. 58–60 on Nikeratos' off-stage wife.
18 See Rosivach 1998: 36–7.
19 Brown 1993, esp. 195–6.
20 Important discussions of metatheatricality in ancient drama include Slater 1985 and 2002, Dobrov 2002 and (with specific ref. to Menander) Gutzwiller 2000 and Petrides 2014.
21 Dobrov 2002: 14–16.
22 Webster, Green and Seeberg 1995: 4–5; Wiles 1991: 188–208.
23 Wiles 1991: 188–9, citing Pollux, *Onomasticon* 4.118–20, Donatus, *On Comedy* 8.7 and archaeological evidence.
24 E.g. Aristotle, *Poetics* 1453a6–22; *Nicomachean Ethics* 1135b12–20.
25 Barigazzi 1965: 148–50, Cinaglia 2012: 557–9.
26 Gutzwiller 2000: 114–27.
27 E.g. Sophocles, *Ajax* 79, 303, 382, 454, *Electra* 1153; Euripides, *Medea* 382, 797, 1049; see Dillon 1991.
28 Plutarch, *On the Fame of the Athenians* 4 (*Moralia* 347e).
29 Plautus, *Casina* 1012–18; cf. Sharrock 2009: 265–6. Similarly, Plautus, *Cistellaria* 782–7 and Terence, *Andria* 980–1 are deliberately perfunctory endings.
30 E.g. *In the Clutches of the Gang* (1914), *Love, Speed and Thrills* (1915), *King, Queen, Joker* (1921), *The Great Dictator* (1940), etc. See King 2002: 43–4; Paulus and King 2010: 222–3. The technique reappears from time to time in later film and television comedy, e.g. Ronnie Barker's *Futtocks End* (1969), *The Benny Hill Show* (BBC Television, 1969–1989).
31 Bentley 1991: 248.
32 Garland 1989: 219–25, Oakley and Sinos 1993.
33 Griffiths 2018: 8–9.
34 See Pelling 2000 on the use of literary texts by Greek historians.
35 See Petrides 2014: 10–20, in contrast to Zagagi 1994: 94–5.
36 Pierce 1997; Sommerstein 2013: 30–36.

37 See www.imdb.com/title/tt0118401 (accessed 16 April 2020).

38 Cf. *Dyskolos* 761–2, 842–4; *Perikeiromene* 1010–15; *Misoumenos* 973–81; cf. Oakley and Sinos 1993: 9–10, Zagagi 1994: 140–1; Sommerstein 2013: 316–17.

39 Oakley and Sinos 1993: 15–16.

40 Cf. Menander frs 908, 910; Posidippus fr. 6. See also Arnott 2000: 184–5 (supplying extra references), Scafuro 2014: 232–4, Bain 1977: 186–7.

Guide to Further Reading

Since his rediscovery Menander has been widely studied and discussed. Many modern editions, commentaries, books and articles are available. The works recommended here represent a fraction of the total, and they inevitably reflect personal preference. Some of the most interesting work on Menander has been done by French and German scholars, so it helps if you can read those languages, but in the list below the main emphasis is on publications in English.

This section is concerned with general and introductory works; the main purpose of the endnotes to the main chapters is to direct readers to specialized bibliography on particular topics or questions of interest.

Editions and commentaries

The Loeb Classical Library edition of Menander by W.G. Arnott is probably the most widely accessible version (*Menander*, vols. I–III, Cambridge, MA, 1979–2000): *Samia* appears in volume III. Arnott's edition contains a parallel English translation and brief notes. Other widely cited editions (which differ from one another in large and small details, including line numbering) include C. Austin, *Menandri Aspis et Samia* (De Gruyter: Berlin, 1969), J.-M. Jacques, *Menandre I.1: La Samienne* (3rd ed., Budé: Paris, 2003) F.H. Sandbach, *Menandri Reliquiae Selectae* (2nd ed., Oxford Classical Texts: Oxford, 1990).

A.H. Sommerstein's edition of *Samia* in the Cambridge University Press 'Green and Yellow' series (Cambridge, 2013) contains the most detailed and up-to-date commentary: it is essential for scholarly purposes but also follows the general aims of that series in providing plenty of basic linguistic help for students. D.C. Bain's edition in the Aris and Phillips series (Warminster, 1983) is somewhat skeletal but full of insight; like all members of that series it includes a parallel English translation. The commentary on the entire extant works of Menander by A.W. Gomme and F.H. Sandbach – *Menander: A Commentary* (Oxford, 1973) – is aimed at the more advanced scholar but contains much that is accessible; it is particularly useful for tracing links and cross-references between *Samia* and other plays.

Translations into English

My own personal preference is for Norma Miller's version in the Penguin Classics (*Menander: Plays and Fragments*, London, 1987), which I have used successfully for teaching purposes: Miller translates Menander into fluent, natural English prose which can be read or spoken without difficulty. David Christenson's more recent prose version, in *Hysterical Laughter: Four Ancient Comedies about Women* (Oxford, 2015) is lively and enjoyable, and would work well in performance. Other translations exist, but readers are advised to avoid anything published before 1969 (unless they are interested in seeing what the fragments of *Samia* looked like before the Bodmer Papyrus came to light). For those who prefer a verse translation, I recommend Eric Turner's elegant and entertaining version, *The Girl from Samos, or The In-Laws* (London, 1972), which was written for performance on BBC Radio Three in 1971 – but be warned that Turner fills in the gaps in the papyrus with freely invented lines of his own. Blank verse translations are also provided by Arnott in his Loeb edition (see above) and Maurice Balme in the Oxford World's Classics series (*Menander: The Plays and Fragments*, Oxford, 2000).

Greek theatre, festivals and performance

For many years the standard reference work has been A.W. Pickard-Cambridge's *Dramatic Festivals of Athens* (3rd ed., Oxford, 1988).

However, since its publication much new evidence has come to light, especially relating to theatre and festivals outside Athens: see now E. Csapo and P. Wilson's monumental three-volume work *A Social and Economic History of the Theatre to 300 BC* (Cambridge, 2020–), though only one volume has yet appeared at the time of writing. Meanwhile E. Csapo and W.J. Slater's sourcebook *The Context of Ancient Drama* (Ann Arbor, 1995) contains a useful selection of sources in translation. Many introductory books on Greek drama tend to be heavily slanted towards fifth-century Athens, but on fourth-century drama and other performance settings see E. Csapo, H.R. Goette, J. Green and P. Wilson (eds), *Greek Theatre in the Fourth Century BC* (Berlin and New York, 2014): this is a wide-ranging collection covering many separate aspects of the topic. The best recent books on Greek performance, though not all relate directly to Menander, include D. Wiles, *Greek Theatre Performance: An Introduction* (Cambridge, 2000) and *The Masks of Menander: Sign and Meaning in Greek and Roman Performance* (Cambridge, 1991); P.E. Easterling and E. Hall (eds), *Greek and Roman Actors: Aspects of an Ancient Profession* (Cambridge, 2002); M. Revermann, *Comic Business* (Oxford, 2006); A. Petrides, *Menander, New Comedy and the Visual* (Cambridge, 2014).

Greek comedy

The best starting points are the *Cambridge Companion to Greek Comedy*, edited by Martin Revermann (Cambridge, 2014) and the *Oxford Handbook to Greek and Roman Comedy*, edited by Michael Fontaine and Adele Scafuro (Oxford, 2014): both of these multi-authored works are packed with information and bibliographic help on almost all aspects of Greek comedy. G. Dobrov (ed.), *Brill's Companion to the Study of Greek Comedy* (Leiden, 2010) is also excellent. Readers who want to place Menander more securely within the context of the development of the comic genre will want to consult J. Rusten (ed.), *The Birth of Comedy: Texts, Documents and Art from Athenian Competitions,*

486–280 (Baltimore, 2011): this book provides a synoptic view of the entire genre from its origins onwards, and consists of a mixture of historical source material and fragments of many lost comic authors (all in English translation), accompanied by helpful discussion. Richard Hunter's book *The New Comedy of Greece and Rome* (Cambridge, 1985) is a useful introduction to the fourth-century Greek comedians and the later Roman comedians who adapted their work: it is particularly good at explaining the formulaic nature of later comedy.

Menander

The definitive critical work on Menander remains to be written. Many excellent books and articles discuss individual plays, or specific aspects of his comic style, but there are few comprehensive book-length studies of Menander as a dramatist. Those who read French will benefit from A. Blanchard's excellent work *La Comédie de Ménandre: Politique, Éthique, Esthétique* (Paris, 2007), a relatively slim volume that succinctly covers a lot of ground. A worthwhile general book in English is Netta Zagagi's *The Art of Menander: Convention, Variation and Originality* (London, 1994): Zagagi's coverage of the topic is selective, and (in my view) she overemphasizes Menander's realism, but she successfully shows how Menander's unique quality derives from his subtle manipulation of comic conventions and formulas. T.B.L. Webster's *Introduction to Menander* (Manchester, 1974) takes a similar approach; Webster's older book *Studies in Menander* (London, 1950) is now out of date but remains a classic piece of literary detective work. Stanley Ireland's Aris and Phillips commentaries on Menander – *The Bad-Tempered Man* (Warminster, 1995) and *The Shield and The Arbitration* (Oxford, 2011) – contain many acute insights in their introductory sections and notes. Alan Sommerstein's *Menander in Contexts* (London, 2014) is an interesting (if somewhat uneven) collection of essays reflecting modern critical approaches.

Critical discussions of *Samia*

H.-D. Blume's *Menanders Samia: Eine Interpretation* (Darmstadt, 1974) is a scene-by-scene analysis of the play, which I have found helpful when writing this Companion. Similarly, Sommerstein's commentary (see above) is full of essential material and critical insights at almost every point, and has guided my own reading. No other book-length discussions of *Samia* exist, but the following articles and chapters can be particularly recommended as general interpretations of the play: E.C. Keuls, 'The *Samia* of Menander: an interpretation of its plot and theme', *ZPE* 10 (1973), 1–20; S. West, 'Notes on the *Samia*', *ZPE* 88 (1991), 11–23; A. Traill, *Women and the Comic Plot in Menander* (Cambridge, 2008), 156–69. See also the general bibliography for many other items.

References

Notes to the reader

(1) Ancient authors' names and titles cited in the endnotes are given in full, but the following abbreviations are used:

CGFPR	C. Austin (ed.), *Comicorum Graecorum Fragmenta in Papyris Reperta* (1973).
FGrHist	F. Jacoby et al. (eds), *Die Fragmente der griechischen Historiker* (1923–)
K–A	R. Kassel and C. Austin (eds), *Poetae Comici Graeci* (1983–)
TrGF	R. Kannicht, B. Snell and S. Radt (eds), *Tragicorum Graecorum Fragmenta* (1971–2004)

(2) The following titles of comedies by Menander are cited in Greek, but it may be helpful to have a list of English equivalents:

Aspis	The Shield
Dyskolos	The Cantankerous Man
Encheiridion	The Dagger
Georgos	The Farmer
Epitrepontes	The Arbitrators
Kolax	The Flatterer
Kubernētai	The Captains
Leukadia	The Woman from Leukas
Messenia	The Woman from Messene
Misoumenos	The Hated Man
Perikeiromene	The Girl with Shorn Hair
Phasma	The Apparition
Plokion	The Necklace
Sikyonios	The Man From Sikyon
Synaristosai	Women Having Lunch Together
Theophoroumenē	The Woman Possessed by a God

Adair, G. 1997. *Surfing the Zeitgeist.* London.
Allinson, F. 1921. (ed.) *Menander: The Principal Fragments.* Cambridge, MA.
Arnott, P. 1959. 'Animals in the Greek theatre', *Greece & Rome* 6: 177–9.
Arnott, W.G. 1979. (ed.) *Menander I.* Cambridge, MA.
Arnott, W.G. 1996. (ed.) *Alexis: The Fragments.* Cambridge.
Arnott, W.G. 1997. 'Humour in Menander', in A. Timonen and V. Rissanen (eds), *Laughter Down the Centuries III.* Turku: 65–79.
Arnott, W.G. 2000. (ed.) *Menander III.* Cambridge, MA.
Arnott, W.G. 2010. 'Middle Comedy', in Dobrov 2010: 279–331.
Bader, B. 'The ψόφος of the house-door in Greek New Comedy', *Antichthon* 5: 35–48.
Bain, D. 1977. *Actors and Audience.* Oxford.
Bain, D. 1981. *Masters, Servants and Orders in Greek Tragedy.* Manchester.
Bain, D. 1983. (ed.) *Menander: Samia.* Warminster.
Bain, D. 1991. 'Six Greek verbs of sexual congress', *Classical Quarterly* 41: 51–77.
Bakola, E., Prauscello, L. and Telò, M. 2013. (eds) *Greek Comedy and the Discourse of Genres.* Cambridge.
Barigazzi, A. 1965. *La formazione spirituale di Menandro.* Turin.
Barthes, R. 1973. *The Pleasure of the Text*, tr. R. Miller. New York.
Bentley, E. 1991. *The Life of Drama.* New York.
Berczelly, L. 1988. 'The date and significance of the Menander mosaics at Mytilene', *Bulletin of the Institute of Classical Studies* 35: 119–26.
Bernabò Brea, L. 1992–3. 'Masks and characters of the Greek theatre in the ancient terracottas of Lipari', *Mediterranean Archaeology* 5–6: 23–31.
Blanchard, A. 2002. 'Moschion *ho kosmios* et l'interpretation de la *Samienne* de Ménandre', *Revue des Etudes Grecques* 115: 58–74.
Blume, H.-D. 1974. *Menanders Samia: Eine Interpretation.* Darmstadt.
Blundell, J. 1980. *Menander and the Monologue.* Göttingen.
Brown, P. 1987. 'Masks, names and characters in New Comedy', *Hermes* 115: 181–202.
Brown, P. 1990. 'Plots and prostitutes in Greek New Comedy', *Papers of the Leeds Latin Seminar* 6: 241–66.
Brown, P. 1993. 'Love and marriage in Greek new comedy', *Classical Quarterly* 43: 189–205.
Byrne, J. 2012. *Writing Comedy*, 4th ed. London.
Capps, E. 1910. *Four Plays of Menander.* Boston.
Carey, C. 1995. 'Rape and adultery in Athenian law', *Classical Quarterly* 45: 407–17.

Carey, C. 2013. 'Rhetoric in (the other) Menander', in C. Kremmydas and K. Tempest (eds), *Hellenistic Oratory*. Oxford: 93–107.

Casanova, A. 2014. 'Menander and the Peripatos: new insights into an old question', in Sommerstein 2014: 137–51.

Charitōnidēs, S., Kahil, L., and Ginouvès, R. 1970. *Les mosaïques de la Maison du Ménandre à Mytilène* (*Antike Kunst*-BH VI). Bern.

Christenson, D. 2000. (ed.) *Plautus: Amphitryo*. Cambridge.

Cinaglia, V. 2012. 'Aristotle and Menander on how people go wrong', *Classical Quarterly* 62: 553–66.

Cinaglia, V. 2014. 'Menander, Aristotle, chance and accidental ignorance', in Sommerstein 2014: 152–66.

Cinaglia, V. 2015. *Aristotle and Menander on the Ethics of Understanding*. Leiden.

Collard, C. 1989. 'Menander, *Samia* 96–115 Sandbach', *Liverpool Classical Monthly* 14: 101–2.

Csapo, E. 1999. 'Performance and iconographic tradition in the illustrations of Menander', *Syllecta Classica* 10: 154–88.

Csapo, E. 2000. 'From Aristophanes to Menander: genre transformation in Greek comedy', in M. Depew and D. Obbink (eds), *Matrices of Genre*. Cambridge, MA: 115–33.

Csapo, E. 2010. *Actors and Icons of the Ancient Theatre*. Chichester.

Csapo, E. and Slater, W.J. 1995. *The Context of Ancient Drama*. Ann Arbor.

Csapo, E. and Wilson, P. 2020. *A Social and Economic History of The Theatre to 300 BC. Volume II: Theatre Beyond Athens*. Cambridge.

Cusset, C. 2003. *Ménandre ou la comédie tragique*. Paris.

Cusset, C. and Lhostis, N. 2011. 'Les maximes dans trois comédies de Ménandre', in Mauduit, C. and Paré-Rey, P. (eds) *Les maximes théâtrales en Grèce et à Rome*. Paris: 93–108.

Dedoussi, C. 1988. 'The future of Plangon's child in Menander's *Samia*', *Liverpool Classical Monthly* 13: 39–42.

Dickey, E. 1996. *Greek Forms of Address*. Oxford.

Dillon, M. 1991. 'Tragic laughter', *Classical World* 84: 345–55.

Dobrov, G. 2002. *Figures of Play*. Oxford and New York.

Dobrov, G. 2010. (ed.) *Brill's Companion to the Study of Greek Comedy*. Leiden.

Duckworth, G. 1994. *The Nature of Roman Comedy*, 2nd ed. Norman.

Dunn, F. 1996. *Tragedy's End*. Oxford.

Fountoulakis, A. 2009. 'Going beyond the Athenian polis: a reappraisal of Menander, *Samia* 96–118', *Quaderni Urbinati di Cultura Classica* 93: 97–117.

Frost, K. 1988. *Exits and Entrances in Menander.* Oxford.
Frye, N. 1957. *Anatomy of Criticism.* Princeton.
Garland, R. 1989. *The Greek Way of Life.* London.
Germany, R. 2014. 'The unity of time in Menander', in Sommerstein 2014: 90–105.
Gomme, A.W. 1936. 'Notes on Menander', *Classical Quarterly* 30: 64–72.
Gomme, A.W. and Sandbach, F.W. 1973 (eds) *Menander: A Commentary.* Oxford.
Goward, B. 1999. *Telling Tragedy.* London.
Grant, J.N. 1986. 'The father–son relationship and the ending of Menander's *Samia*', *Phoenix* 40: 172–84.
Green, J.R. 1994. *Theatre in Ancient Greek Society.* London.
Green, P. 1990. *Alexander to Actium.* Berkeley.
Griffiths, E. 2018. *If Not Critical.* Oxford.
Gutzwiller, K. 2000. 'The tragic mask of comedy: metatheatricality in Menander', *Classical Antiquity* 19: 102–37.
Hall, E.M. 1995. 'Lawcourt dramas: the power of performance in Greek forensic oratory', *Bulletin of the Institute of Classical Studies* 40: 39–58.
Halliwell, S.J. 2008. *Greek Laughter.* Cambridge.
Hamilton, E. 1932. *The Greek Way.* New York.
Harding, D.W. 1998. *Regulated Hatred and Other Essays on Jane Austen*, ed. M. Lawlor. London.
Hardwick, L. 2000. *Translating Words, Translating Cultures.* London.
Heap, A. 2003. 'The baby as hero? The role of the infant in Menander', *Bulletin of the Institute of Classical Studies* 46: 77–129.
Henderson, J. 1975. *The Maculate Muse.* New Haven.
Henderson, J. 1991. 'Women and the Athenian dramatic festivals', *Transactions of the American Philological Association* 121: 133–47.
Holzberg, N. 1974. *Menander: Untersuchungen zur dramatischen Technik.* Nuremberg.
Hurst, A. 1990. 'Ménandre et la tragédie', in E. Handley and A. Hurst (eds), *Relire Ménandre.* Geneva: 93–122.
Hytner, N. 2017. *Balancing Acts: Behind the Scenes at the National Theatre.* London.
Ireland, S. 1981. 'Prologues, structure and sentences in Menander', *Hermes* 109: 178–88.
Ireland, S. 1983. 'Menander and the comedy of disappointment', *Liverpool Classical Monthly* 8: 45–7.

Ireland, S. 1994. 'Personal relationships and other features of Menander', *Electronic Antiquity* 24 [online].

Issacharoff, M. 1981. 'Space and reference in drama', *Poetics Today* 2: 211–24.

Jackson, L. 2020. *The Chorus of Drama in the Fourth Century* BCE. Oxford.

Jacques, J.-M. 2003. (ed.) *Menandre: La Samienne*, 3rd ed. Paris.

Jäkel, S. 1982. 'Euripideische Handlungsstrukturen in der *Samia* des Menander', *Arctos* 16: 19–31.

Josipovici, G. 2016. *Hamlet, Fold on Fold.* New Haven.

Kasser, R. and Austin, C. 1969. *Papyrus Bodmer XXV. Ménandre: La Samienne.* Cologny.

Katsouris, A.G. 1975a. *Tragic Patterns in Menander.* Athens.

Katsouris, A.G. 1975b. *Linguistic and Stylistic Characterization: Tragedy and Menander.* Thessaloniki.

Kawin, B. 1972. *Telling It Again and Again: Repetition in Literature and Film.* Ithaca.

Kermode, F. 1967. *The Sense of an Ending.* Oxford.

Keuls, E. 1973. 'The *Samia* of Menander: an interpretation of its plot and theme', *Zeitschrift für Papyrologie und Epigraphik* 10: 1–20.

King, G. 2002. *Film Comedy.* London.

Konstan, D. 1993. 'The young concubine in Menandrian comedy', in R. Scodel (ed.), *Theater and Society in the Classical World.* Ann Arbor: 139–60.

Konstan, D. 2013. 'Menander's slaves: the banality of violence', in B. Akrigg and R. Tordoff (eds), *Slaves and Slavery in Ancient Greek Comic Drama.* Cambridge: 144–58.

Körte, A. 1932. 'Menandros', in A. Pauly, G. Wissowa and W. Kroll (eds), *Realencyclopädie der classischen Altertumswissenschaft*, vol. XV. Stuttgart: 707–61.

Krieter-Spiro, M. 1997. *Sklaven, Köche und Hetären: Das Dienstpersonal bei Menander.* Stuttgart.

Lape, S. 2004. *Reproducing Athens.* Princeton.

Lape, S. and Moreno, A. 2014. 'Comedy and the social historian', in Revermann 2014: 336–69.

Lefebvre, G. 1907. *Fragments d'un manuscrit de Ménandre.* Cairo.

Lefkowitz, M. 2012. *The Lives of the Greek Poets*, 2nd ed. Baltimore.

Liapis, V. 2002. (ed.) *Menandrou gnomai monostichoi.* Athens.

Lloyd-Jones, H. 1972. 'Menander's *Samia* in the light of the new evidence', *Yale Classical Studies* 22: 119–44.

Loraux, N. 1987. *Tragic Ways of Killing a Woman*, tr. A. Forster. Cambridge, MA.

Lowe, J. 1962. 'The manuscript evidence for changes of speaker in Aristophanes', *Bulletin of the Institute of Classical Studies* 9: 27–42.

Lowe, N. 2000. *The Classical Plot and the Invention of Western Narrative*. Cambridge.

Lowe, N. 2007. *Comedy*. Cambridge.

MacCary, W. 1970. 'Menander's characters: their names, roles and masks', *Transactions of the American Philological Association* 100: 277–94.

MacCary, W. 1972. 'Menander's soldiers: their names, roles and masks', *American Journal of Philology* 93: 279–98.

Maidment, K.J. 1935. 'The later comic chorus', *Classical Quarterly* 29: 1–24.

Major, W. 1997. 'Menander in a Macedonian world', *Greek, Roman and Byzantine Studies* 38: 41–74.

Marshall, C.W. 2006. *The Stagecraft and Performance of Roman Comedy*. Cambridge.

Mette, H. 1969. 'Moschion, *ho kosmios*', *Hermes* 97: 432–9.

Miller, D.A. 1981. *Narrative and its Discontents*. Princeton.

Munteanu, D. 2002. 'Types of anagnorisis: Aristotle and Menander', *Wiener Studien* 115: 111–26.

Nervegna, S. 2013. *Menander in Antiquity*. Cambridge.

Nesselrath, H.-G. 1990. *Die attische mittlere Komödie*. Berlin.

Nünlist, R. 2002. 'Speech within speech in Menander', in Willi 2002: 19–59.

Oakley, J. and Sinos, R. 1993. *The Wedding in Ancient Athens*. Madison.

Ogden, D. 1996. *Greek Bastardy*. Oxford.

Omitowoju, R. 2002. *Rape and the Politics of Consent in Classical Athens*. Cambridge.

Parker, R. 1996. *Athenian Religion: A History*. Oxford.

Parker, R. 2005. *Polytheism and Society at Athens*. Oxford.

Paulus, T. and King, R. 2010. *Slapstick Comedy*. London.

Pelling, C.B. 2000. *Literary Texts and the Greek Historian*. London.

Petersmann, H. 1971. 'Philologische Untersuchungen zur antiken Bühnentür', *Wiener Studien* 5: 91–109.

Petrides, A. 2014. *Menander, New Comedy and the Visual*. Cambridge.

Pickard-Cambridge, A. 1988. *The Dramatic Festivals of Athens*, 3rd ed. Oxford.

Pierce, K. 1997. 'The portrayal of rape in New Comedy', in S. Deacy and K. Pierce (eds) *Rape in Antiquity*. London and Swansea: 163–84.

Poe, J.P. 1996. 'The supposed conventional meanings of dramatic masks: a re-examination of Pollux 4.133–54', *Philologus* 140: 306–28.
Pohlmann, E. and West, M.L. 2002. *Documents of Ancient Greek Music*. Oxford.
Porter, J. 2006. (ed.) *Classical Pasts*. Princeton.
Porter, J.R. 1997. 'Adultery by the book: Lysias 1 and comic diegesis', *Echos du Monde Classique* 40: 421–53.
Pütz, B. 2014. 'Good to laugh with: animals in comedy', in G. Campbell (ed.), *The Oxford Handbook of Animals in Classical Thought and Life*. Oxford: 61–72.
Revermann, M. 2014. (ed.) *The Cambridge Companion to Greek Comedy*. Cambridge.
Romero-Trillo, J. 2013. 'Pragmatic markers', *Encyclopedia of Applied Linguistics*. Malden and Oxford.
Rosen, R. 2012. 'Timocles fr. 6 and the parody of Greek literary theory', in C.W. Marshall and G. Kovacs (eds), *No Laughing Matter*. London: 177–86.
Rosivach, V. 1998. *When A Young Man Falls in Love*. London.
Rothwell, K. 1995. 'The continuity of the chorus in fourth-century Attic comedy', in G. Dobrov (ed.), *Beyond Aristophanes*. Atlanta: 99–118.
Rothwell, K. 2007. *Nature, Culture and the Origins of Greek Comedy*. Cambridge.
Rutherford, R. 2012. *Greek Tragic Style*. Cambridge.
Sandbach, F.H. 1970. 'Menander's manipulation of language for dramatic purposes', in Turner 1970: 113–36.
Sandbach, F.H. 1986. 'Two notes on Menander', *Liverpool Classical Monthly* 11: 156–60.
Scafuro, A. 1997. *The Forensic Stage*. Cambridge.
Scafuro, A. 2003. 'When a gesture was misinterpreted: *didonai titthion* in Menander's *Samia*', in G.W. Bakewell and J. Sickinger (eds), *Gestures: Essays in Ancient History, Literature and Philosophy*. Oxford: 113–35.
Scafuro, A. 2014. 'Menander', in M. Fontaine and A. Scafuro (eds), *The Oxford Handbook to Greek and Roman Comedy*. Oxford: 218–38.
Schlueter, J. 1995. *Dramatic Closure: Reading the End*. Madison.
Schwindt, J. 1994. *Das Motiv der Tagesspanne: Ein Beitrag zur Ästhetik der Zeitgestaltung im griechisch-römischen Drama*. Paderborn.
Sharrock, A. 2009. *Reading Roman Comedy*. Cambridge.
Sidwell, K. 2000. 'From old to middle to new? Aristotle's *Poetics* and the history of Athenian comedy,' in F.D. Harvey and J.M. Wilkins (eds), *The Rivals of Aristophanes*. London and Swansea: 247–58.

Simmons, E.J. 1962. *Chekhov: A Biography.* Chicago.

Slater, N.W. 1985. *Plautus in Performance.* Princeton.

Slater, N.W. 2002. *Spectator Politics.* Philadelphia.

Small, J.P. 2013. '*Skenographia* in brief', in G. Harrison and V. Liapis (eds), *Performance in Greek and Roman Theatre*, Leiden: 111–28.

Sommerstein, A.H. 2006. 'Rape and consent in Athenian tragedy', in D.L. Cairns and V. Liapis (eds), *Dionysalexandros: Essays on Aeschylus and his Fellow Tragedians.* London and Swansea: 233–51.

Sommerstein, A.H. 2010. 'The titles of Greek comedies', in *The Tangled Ways of Zeus.* Oxford: 11–29.

Sommerstein, A.H. 2013. (ed.) *Menander: Samia.* Cambridge.

Sommerstein, A.H. 2014. (ed.) *Menander in Contexts.* London.

Stoessl, F. 1969. 'Die neuen Menanderpublikationen der Bibliotheca Bodmeriana', *Rheinisches Museum für Philologie* 112: 193–229.

Storey, I.C. 2011. *Fragments of Old Comedy*, 3 vols. Cambridge, MA.

Sutherland, J. 2005. *Inside Bleak House.* London.

Taplin, O. 1977. 'Did Greek dramatists write stage directions?' *Papers of the Cambridge Philological Society* 23: 121–32.

Tarn, W.J. 1952, *Hellenistic Civilization*, 3rd ed. London.

Traill, A. 2008. *Women and the Comic Plot in Menander.* Cambridge.

Treu, K. 1969. 'Humane Handlungsmotive in der *Samia* Menanders', *Rheinisches Museum für Philologie* 112: 230–54.

Treu, K. 1981. 'Menanders Menschen als Polisbürger', *Philologus* 125: 211–14.

Turner, E. 1970. (ed.) *Ménandre.* Geneva.

Voelke, P. 2012. 'Les failles de la *kosmiotês* dans la *Samienne* de Ménandre', *Revue de philologie, de littérature et d'histoire anciennes* 86: 123–41.

Vogt-Spira, G. 1992. *Dramaturgie des Zufalls. Tyche und Handeln in der Komödie Menanders.* Munich.

Webster, T.B.L. 1950. *Studies in Menander.* Manchester.

Webster, T.B.L. 1970. *Studies in Later Greek Comedy*, 2nd ed. Manchester.

Webster, T.B.L., Green, R. and Seeberg, A. 1995. *Monuments Illustrating New Comedy*, 3rd ed. London.

Weissenberger, M. 1991. 'Vater-Sohn Beziehung und Komödienhandlung in Menanders *Samia*', *Hermes* 119: 415–34.

Weitz, E. 2009. *The Cambridge Introduction to Comedy.* Cambridge.

West, M.L. 1987. *An Introduction to Greek Metre.* Oxford.

West, M.L. 1992. *Ancient Greek Music.* Oxford.

West, S. 1991. 'Notes on the *Samia*'. *Zeitschrift für Philologie und Epigraphik* 88: 11–23.

Wiles, D. 1991. *The Masks of Menander.* Cambridge.

Wiles, D. 1997. *Tragedy in Athens.* Cambridge.

Wiles, D. 2000. *Greek Theatre Performance: An Introduction.* Cambridge.

Wiles, D. 2007. *Mask and Performance in Greek Tragedy.* Cambridge.

Wilkins, J.M. 2000. *The Boastful Chef.* Oxford.

Willi, A. 2002. (ed.) *The Language of Greek Comedy.* Oxford.

Wright, M.E. 2012. *The Comedian as Critic.* London.

Wright, M.E. 2013. 'Poets and poetry in later Greek comedy', *Classical Quarterly* 63: 603–22.

Wright, M.E. forthcoming. 'Wisdom in inverted commas: Greek comedy and the quotable maxim', in M.E. Wright (ed.), *Classical Literature and Quotation Culture.*

Zagagi, N. 1994. *The Comedy of Menander.* London.

Index

Entries highlighted with an asterisk (*) represent principal topics, characters or themes which are discussed in detail.